Successful Real Estate Investing

Successful Real Estate Investing

How to Avoid the 75 Most Costly Mistakes Every Investor Makes

ROBERT SHEMIN

WILEY

John Wiley & Sons, Inc.

Published by John Wiley & Sons, Inc., Hoboken, New Jersey.
Published simultaneously in Canada.

For general information on our other products and services please contact our Customer Care Department within the United States at (800) 762-2974, outside the United States at (317) 572-3993 or fax (317) 572-4002.

Wiley also publishes its books in a variety of electronic formats. Some content that appears in print may not be available in electronic books. For more information about Wiley products, visit our web site at *www.Wiley.com*.

Library of Congress Cataloging-in-Publication Data

Shemin, Robert, 1963–
    Successful real estate investing : how to avoid the 75 most costly mistakes every investor makes / Robert Shemin.
        p. cm.
    Includes index.
    ISBN 0-471-45397-8 (pbk.)
      1. Real estate investment.   I. Title.
HD1382.5.S468 2003
332.63'24—dc22   2003063151

Printed in the United States of America

10 9 8 7 6 5 4 3 2 1

To my son Alexander—the biggest mistake I've made in my life is not spending MORE time with you. No matter how much time we spend together, it's not enough.

CONTENTS

Contents

Contents

Contents

Contents

ACKNOWLEDGMENTS

Thank you, Michael Hamilton and all of the great people at John Wiley & Sons, Inc., for helping me create such great books. Kimberly Vaughn makes it all happen.

As always, none of this would be possible without the support of my parents, Lill and Jules Shemin. Thank you, Patricia, for your constant help, support, and patience. Paul Bauer, Jeff Vikari, Danny Wagner, and all of the great people at the Creative Real Estate Institute and PMG: You all deserve a million thanks. Rosemary Taugher, Evelyn Levenson, and Chelsea Taugher-Dias actually do all of my work—I just sit back and watch.

This book is actually written and edited by Barbara McNichol, who is called my editor, but is so much more.

A special thanks to the people who have given me great speaking opportunities: Wright Thurston and Peter Conti, Vera Jones-Cox, Dwan and Sharon, the Learning Annex, the National Association of Real Estate Investors, Troy Titus, Albert Aiello, and the giant of real estate investing, William Kartz.

Furthermore, thanks to all of my students and friends who helped remind me of the mistakes I make. Tamara Davis, you help me more than I help you. Thanks also to Andrea Morris, Jonathan Schwandt,

Steve Smith, Jack Chen, Brad Chandler, Jonathan McNamara, Michael Pope, Gregory Kowert, and Hoert and John D. Vincent.

Also, some of the best advice I get for business and life comes from Kabbalah. Thank you to Paul and Karen Burg, all of the people at the center, and especially Abraham Kellerman.

Thank you, Jack Bufkin, for still taking my calls.

Successful Real Estate Investing

Ten years ago, I had no desire to be in real estate. I was in financial consulting. One day I was referred to an older couple in Nashville, Tennessee. I went to this dumpy home office where they worked. Outside was a beat-up old pickup—not a good sign that they'd be able to afford my financial products and services.

This couple, then in their seventies, had started investing in real estate when they were in their early fifties. The man didn't own a computer then and still doesn't today. (We love to complicate things in real estate, yet it doesn't require sophisticated technology.) As I was leaving their office, I told them they were the nicest people I'd met, but they clearly weren't qualified to work with our consulting firm. Although I didn't say it, I thought it: They looked broke.

Then he stopped me and offered to show me his accounting book. His handwritten ledgers indicated that he owned 120 houses, all paid for. That meant his net worth was *at least* $6 million, assuming the value of each house was only $50,000. Next, he showed me he had $85,000 coming in each month, netting $60,000 after expenses. He looked me in the eye and said, "Robert, my wife and I have been taking six-month vacations for several years. How's your job?"

All of a sudden, I got interested in real estate. I thought, if this guy can do this volume with no computer, no sophistication, no real education or background, maybe I've got a chance. Since then, I've traveled around the country and met all types of investors. I've learned that the most successful investors are like this man: They keep it simple.

Anyhow, I decided to go into investing. For the first year, I followed the man around, learned from other investors, and read books—educating myself as thoroughly as I could. I thought and worried and ran in circles all day. And guess how much money I made? None. But I was busy and stressed out. Ever get focused on the wrong activities? Well, in that first year, I didn't make any offers, and I didn't buy any real estate. Have you tried that method? It works! I promise you: If you don't make offers, you won't get any real estate—guaranteed! So if you're just getting started, or having a bad month, or experiencing a bad year, the solution is simple: Make more offers.

I have a rare form of dyslexia: I can read, but I can't type. I also have no sense of direction: I can't read a map. I cannot put a three-year-old child's toy together. I have no spatial abilities. Working in real estate, it would help if I could use a computer and had a sense of direction. I can't and don't. In fact, when I bought my first duplex, I couldn't even find it. I spent four days looking for it until I finally got over my pride and called the broker who sold it to me. He had to help me find it. Still, within one year, I bought 12 duplexes while keeping my job. Over the past 10 years, I have developed 52 ways of finding good deals in real estate. Foreclosures, divorces, estate sales, short sales, For Rent ads, driving for dollars, aging landlords who are tired of landlording—and that's just a summary. You can pick one or two or three of these, and if you work them consistently, you'll find deals. (See Appendix A.)

Three Elements of Success in Real Estate

The number-one determinant of success is *what you believe.* You must continually educate yourself to boost your belief that you can make big money in real estate. I promise, on your fiftieth wholesale deal, your belief will be a lot stronger than on your first or second deal. The second determinant for success is *know-how,* and the third is *consistent action.*

Belief, know-how, and consistent action. Most people, including myself, fail at consistent action. They won't make the number of calls, look at the houses, make the number of offers it takes, and simply stick with it.

Given that, I challenge you to stick with real estate as an investment business for five years, then make a decision. Have you ever met anyone who's been successful at something they've worked at for only three weeks? Here's an example. On January 5, the gym I go to was packed with 200 people. Each of them showed belief and know-how about getting fit. But on January 25, only 50 people were at the same gym. Those who quit showing up lacked the third element for success— consistent action. If you're not getting what you want, make sure you're committed in these three areas.

Make Lots of Offers

I have also become a teacher of real estate investment through my seminars. They help me learn more and more about this business.

One of my students in Ohio said she couldn't become an investor because she's shy and doesn't like talking to people. I told her she could still succeed at investing in real estate by making mass offers through the mail. Now she combs through expired listings and sends out 100 offers a week. She uses a sample contract from my real estate course and types in the address and the offer price very systematically. The contract has a contingency clause, so if some of the details don't work out, she doesn't have to buy the property. The clause says "contingent on buyer's inspection and approval before closing." If the sellers list the house for $300,000, she needs to offer at least 25 percent below what it's worth, or $225,000. But to keep things even simpler, she divides by 2. If they're asking $300,000, she might offer $150,000.

Some time ago, I paid $8,000 to spend four hours with one of the top Realtors in the United States. Terry lists and sells 900 houses a year. He told me that he never makes "even" offers; he always uses odd numbers. This means that if he's listing a house for sale and it's worth $500,000, he lists it for $497,836. He does this to make sure the listing comes under certain parameters. For example, if someone does a computer search for "houses under $500,000," his property falls into that group. Plus, when he's negotiating, people think he knows something important. "Why'd you offer $497,836?" they ask. He replies, "I've got a program." They're impressed. So try Terry's method and make odd-number offers. If it's good enough for this successful investor, it's good enough for us.

Adopting this advice, the Ohio student mentioned before sends out 100 odd-number offers a week. For example, if the sellers are asking $300,000, she offers $149,817. It takes her about an hour and 15 minutes to send out 100 offers a week, and it costs her $40 in postage. Of the offers she sends, 95 percent aren't even acknowledged. With 3 to 4 percent of her offers, the sellers or real estate agents actually call her up and cuss her out, saying, "I can't stand you investors. You offer ridiculous prices." Then they hang up.

But about 1 percent of her offers go into play. Using this method for just a year and a half, she located a number of highly motivated sellers and now owns 110 properties. I suggest you follow her lead and simply make more offers.

In my second year in real estate, I made a handful of offers. Unfortunately, the offer I made on 4658 Forest Ridge Drive was accepted. When your first offer is accepted, it's a nightmare; now you're really in the business of real estate investing, and it can be frightening. But clearly there's much to be learned—such as how to invest with no money of your own.

Using Other People's Money

When I started, I had no cash and no credit. In fact, my parents had taught me never to borrow money, so I never had any credit. Banks wouldn't lend money to me. I found out quickly that what's worse than *bad* credit is having no credit at all. Today, I have tenants who have filed for Chapter 13 bankruptcy, and my office can still get home loans for them. But back then, without any credit record, banks said I didn't exist. I was 28 years old and was making good money, but I'd spent it all. Fortunately, I had to find other ways to buy property, simply because I had no money or credit of my own.

You have a choice: You can use your own money and credit to buy property, or you can use *other people's money* (OPM). There's nothing wrong with using your own funds. But you can do what many investors have done, as I have done in my last 200 transactions. I didn't use one penny of my own money or one point of my own credit, thanks to the creative financing techniques that exist out there. You can learn them, too.

Treat Investing as a Real Business

Job security is a rare thing these days, so it's wise to start your own business. People might say there's no job security in real estate, that it's a high-risk profession. Yet they could be laid off from their corporate jobs tomorrow through no fault of their own. Real estate investing can provide a safety net.

I challenge you to start your own business, even if you do it on the side part-time, as I did starting out. Working for someone else is like going to the gym five times a week, but your boss builds all the muscle.

When I was 28, I owned 12 duplexes, and because I was making $3,600 a month net, I decided to retire. Rental property is the best wealth builder, if you can put up with the headaches. If you're putting $3,600 a month in your pocket from rental properties, you pay little or no tax because of depreciation and write-offs. And because you have a business, you can write off all of your business-related education, travel, office, car, and phone expenses. Start thinking about after-tax dollars. If you'd like to get a Hummer H2 tax-free, you can buy it and write off its cost the first year you own it. When you work for someone else's business, you can't do that. If you're making $3,600 after taxes from rental property, how much would you have to make at a *real* job to put $3,600 in your pocket? Estimate it at $5,000 or $6,000 plus the income-tax withholding, federal and state payroll taxes, and all that.

I started with 12 duplexes, then 20, then 50, and then 100. At one time, I was up to 300 properties. I'm now down to 148. I've bought and sold 75 properties in the past five months. I'm also working on my biggest transaction ever: I'll be putting a commercial building worth $7 million under contract, with no money down and four months to close. I got it at 30 cents on the dollar in Memphis, Tennessee.

I love teaching. And I have three best-selling books, with more coming out. Even so, I made more from one real estate deal in South Florida a few months ago than I made from all my book royalties and all my course sales. The money is in real estate. I love teaching and helping people, but I make my money in real estate.

I'm from Nashville and live in South Beach, Florida, where people told me there were no deals. There may not be, but I've flipped four high-end condos in the past 90 days, and I'm doing lease options. It's competitive, but the deals are there if you're willing to work.

Sure, I'd like to have a great way to make a lot of money without working, but I've been looking for years. It doesn't exist. In real estate, you *can* make a lot of money, but it still takes effort, just like any other business. It does get easier as you go, and compared with other businesses, it's more fun and more profitable. After all, more than 90 percent of the millionaires in America earned their money in real estate.

Finding Good Deals

Say you found a property worth $80,000 and you can buy it for $60,000 because you've found a seller who's motivated due to a divorce, estate sale, short sale, foreclosure, or poor maintenance. People find properties like that every day, and you can, too. If you borrow the entire $60,000 to buy something worth $80,000, your net worth goes up $20,000, which is one of your goals. Possibly the hardest thing to understand in real estate is this: You've got to find good deals, because that's how you make money in real estate. It's about the numbers; take the emotion out of your deals.

Say you borrowed $60,000 to buy that $80,000 house. You rent it for $1,000 a month, and your mortgage, taxes, and insurance cost $500. That leaves you with $200 to $300 in your pocket, not the $500 you'd expect. You'll never make as much money from rental property as you'd think, because vacancies and repairs take about 30 percent of the income generated right off the top. Yet even if you have a bad month and only net $150, your return on investment is *infinite*. You have none of your own money invested, yet you make $150—and that can be called an infinite return. Not 10 percent, not 100 percent, but infinite.

Sometimes stockbrokers call and tell me they have a mutual fund that lost 20 percent last year, but this year, they're hoping it will go up 15 percent. I ask if they have an infinite-return mutual fund—one I don't have to put money into, but money keeps coming out. That's real estate; there is no other investment that lets you do that.

Think about what one extra deal is worth to you. Your net worth and cash flow are great, but you may need cash today. What if you found a deal worth $280,000 and put it under contract for $190,000? You could find someone who would pay $218,000 for something worth $280,000; you didn't buy it or borrow money. You found a deal, put it together, and flipped it or wholesaled it and made $28,000 because that's what you get paid for—finding a good deal. What if you found a property that would be worth $75,000 after it's been repaired? You put it under contract for $45,000. If someone is willing to pay you even $50,000, you just made $5,000 for *finding* a good deal. That's called *wholesaling*.

Say you buy one or two rental properties a year and put up with the tenants and their needs. After 10 to 15 years, you (through your tenants' rents) have paid for those properties. The debt on them decreases and their value increases. If you had 10 rental properties in the $100,000 range and you slugged it out—it's work, there'll be headaches—in 15 years, your net worth would increase by at least $1 million. And that's if the property values don't even go up! Look at the history of appreciation in your area. For example, over the past eight years, all the property values in South Florida doubled. Over the next 15 to 20 years, they'll probably double again.

Overcoming Fear and Pride

If you're not getting what you want in life, it's for one of two reasons: fear or pride.

Are you saying things like, "Why should I go wholesale a house? I've never done it, and I'm scared." Now ask yourself: When has fear served you? Or have you ever said, "I'm too good to send out 100 envelopes a week. I'm too smart for that."

If you're not getting what you want in real estate or in life, see if fear or pride is holding you back. Get clear. Decide what action to take. Take a step. Make an offer. Go for it.

Two years ago in a seminar, I asked the participants to stand up and clap. One 21-year-old man named Shad stood on the table and jumped up and down. Obviously he had no fear or pride to stop him from doing that. Shad bought my course that day. In six weeks, he made $7,000 wholesaling a property. After being in real estate for a year and a half, his net worth rose to $1 million. He hasn't borrowed one penny—instead, he has lease-optioned and wholesaled all of his properties.

Why did Shad succeed when others in the seminar did not? After all, he had no real estate experience; he was an $8-an-hour telemarketer. The difference was *action*. Shad said, "I don't know anything about real estate; just tell me what to do and I'll do it." He got the course and did what it said.

At one seminar I gave, a woman hugged me and asked to have her photo taken with me. Two years before, she bought my book *Secrets of a Millionaire Investor,* then bought my old course a year later. Within six weeks of taking action, she wholesaled a property and made $8,000. Then, on her second deal, she made $7,000. As we talked, she started shaking and crying, and she showed me the closing statement and check on her third deal—she made $240,000 (after splitting it with a partner; together, they made over $500,000). She had been making $40,000 a year as a schoolteacher. Now she was a millionaire.

Real Estate Courses

I offer a number of courses to help beginners get started in real estate investing. To me, Real Estate Number 1 is the most important course today in real estate investing. Included are simple action plans based on a part-time, eight-hour work week. It shows you how to talk to sellers, how to analyze properties, how to put them under contract, and how to make money in a variety of ways. It helps you decide on the best way for you to make money.

Once you find a deal, Real Estate Number 2 shows you how to analyze it in 20 minutes or less, in town or out of town. You receive a CD-ROM with all the policies and procedures, all the forms and contracts, and 288 documents, including a land trust that cost me $5,000 initially. Also included is a contract that I paid an attorney $3,000 to review. This course outlines ways to control a property beyond the usual contract: options, lease options, and contract for deed. With three or four more ways to control a property, your rate of closing deals goes up.

The course covers how to analyze properties, how to wholesale from A to Z, how to lease option, how to find properties and control them, how to find buyers, how to go to closing, and how to get property with no money down. All of your questions are answered in this course.

Real Estate Number 3 includes advanced lease optioning, advanced wholesaling, advanced financing, ways to negotiate, ways to control property without using your own money, and advanced management systems. It comes with a workbook and speed tapes to get you jump-started. It provides all the forms you'll need on a CD-ROM.

In Courses 2 and 3, I challenge advanced investors to learn how to make a full-price offer on a property and still make money. That will give you more opportunities to get property. In fact, I'm in the process of getting this creative financing technique trademarked and copyrighted.

Homes for the Homeless

I give proceeds from my books and courses and some real estate to homeless families. Every year, I take at least one of my deals and lease-option a homeless family (usually a single mother) that's been living in a shelter. I help people go from homelessness to homeownership in one year. Maybe you can do the same. You don't have to lose money or give the house away, but you *can* create new homeowners.

Giving houses away is my favorite thing to do, because I believe that in the wealthiest, most powerful nation in the world, it's ridiculous that anyone, especially a child, has to go to bed in a shelter.

PART I

75 Real Mistakes to Avoid in Real Estate

Following are 75 real mistakes that investors (including me) have made in their real estate careers. In sharing these with you, my first goal is to help you increase your business so you make more money. My second goal is to do so by encouraging you to avoid these mistakes. When you do, I guarantee you will save yourself time, money, and headaches.

It's taken me more than 10 years to make these mistakes, so if I can shave time off your learning curve, then I've accomplished something important. Many of these mistakes lead to making policies and procedures that work. I highly recommend you make them part of your policy and procedure manual.

Keep this book on your desk and review the mistakes every week or two. You may be surprised by how many mistakes you're still making.

Mistake # 1

Not Getting Started
in Real Estate Investing Early Enough

My biggest business regret is that I didn't start investing in real estate until I was 28 years old. If someone had told me about it when I was younger, I'd be much further ahead today. One of my youngest students, Chris, bought my course and put two properties under contract in the first six weeks. The first one closed quickly because he ran an ad in the paper and found a buyer who had cash. He made $4,800 net. (He could have made $5,500, but he incurred some costs, which he would have avoided if he'd listened to the rest of the course.) Chris called me from the closing table and immediately said, "I should have started this sooner." His mother had come to the seminar with him, had bought the course for him, and had to sign the contracts, because he was only 16 years old.

David was 58 years old and had just been laid off from his job with no pension. He came to one of my seminars, bought one of my courses, and liked the concept of lease optioning. He completed a few deals very quickly. On the first deal, he lease-optioned a house from a motivated landlord for $105,000. The home was worth $130,000, so he optioned it to the end buyers for $133,000. His mortgage payment was $900 a month, but he was collecting a market rent of $1,400, so he was putting $500 in his pocket every month. I taught him how to negotiate with the landlord to put zero down because the house needed a few repairs. He put no option money down (easy for David because he *had* no money), and he collected $5,500 in

option money from the end buyer. Then I showed him how to arrange it so his first lease payment wouldn't come due for the first 90 days.

In 30 days, David collected his first lease payment and had the option money, and he made $6,000 off one lease option. He called me from the closing table in tears, saying he wished he'd started sooner. He asked me to tell this story every time I speak. The lesson is this: The time to get started is now.

Mistake # 2

Not Paying Attention to the Cycles of Real Estate: Prices, Price Increases, and Price Decreases

Real estate goes through cycles. Some cycles are short, some are long. Sometimes we experience a state close to equilibrium—that's when there are just enough houses and just enough people wanting to buy them. Rents stay the same; prices stay the same. This is extremely rare; the only factor that really drives any market is supply and demand—that is, there are more houses for sale than there are people to buy them, or, conversely, there are fewer houses for sale than there are buyers.

When the demand for housing is high, we're in a growth phase. The main thing that will increase demand for housing is an increase in jobs. An increase in the number of jobs means people will be moving into an area to claim those jobs. To find out about cycles in your area, call your local chamber of commerce or read your business paper and find out how the job market is faring. If your city is losing a lot of jobs, it follows that the housing market will soften or decline.

There's also a hypergrowth phase in which people move in, rents and prices go up, and builders come to town because the revitalized neighborhoods need more rental units. Then there's an oversupply of housing, and the market goes into decline.

If you're considering long-term investing, find out what the job and growth prospects are for your area. They're related to supply and demand in the economy. Apartment associations and national real estate associations usually keep good records on these trends. You don't need to spend a lot of time researching these cycles, but be aware of them.

Mistake # 3

Not Becoming Active in Your Local Real Estate Investors Association

I think belonging to this association is the best deal going. Nearly all of the contacts you need to make can be made there—contractors, closing attorneys, good eviction attorneys, and other investors attend the meetings. You can meet them and build your team based on these contacts.

Going to a monthly real estate meeting is like going to a religious institution on a regular basis. You already know what's going to be said and how the stories end, so why keep going, right? It's because when you do attend, your belief system is reinforced (or challenged), and you meet others with common interests who may change your life. At a minimum, you feel better because you're supporting your beliefs, and theirs, too.

You attend your association meetings for the same reasons. Someone stands up and tells a story about finding a house through the letter carrier; another made $100,000 on an apartment building, and so on. As you listen, you realize—hey, this stuff works! He did it this way and she did it that way— maybe I can do it, too. And now I'm with people who can help me do it.

I spent two years trying to meet all the other landlords and investors in my area, and I found a lot of them. Then, one day, I stumbled into the local real estate investors association. Guess who was there? Everyone I had met—100 investors, 20 landlords, the attorneys, the mortgage brokers, the contractors—they all went to the meetings on a regular basis.

Mistake # 4

Thinking about Short-Term Results Instead of Long-Term Results When Starting Your Real Estate Investment Business

If you get into any business, particularly real estate, get in for the long run. If you don't make at least a five-year commitment to your business, don't even bother getting started. I've never met anyone who got into a business for less than a year and did well. When I started, I made a commitment to work at it part-time for five years; after that, I would decide whether I'd continue. I recommend you make a commitment to yourself and to your clients.

Know that in your second and third years, things begin to happen. People start calling you with deals. You know how to do deals quicker and better. You get very active as an investor.

I've been investing in real estate for 10 years, and I'm now working on the best deal I've ever found. It came to me by accident. "Accidents" will happen to you when you're out doing plenty of activities. Once you get this machine going—finding properties, finding deals, driving for dollars, learning how to wholesale and lease option, doing the rental business, and forming partnerships—all this will snowball. I promise you, it gets to be easier, better, and more fun.

I work with partners in a lot of real estate deals. They put up the money, and we split the profit 50-50. For example, Michael will put up $50,000 on a house that we'll fix and sell for $80,000. We plan to make $30,000 and split it 50-50. Michael would be happy making $15,000 on the $50,000 he borrowed. When we do the deal together, it goes better, and we make $35,000, with Michael getting half.

Here's my way of working. I call him and say, "Michael, here's your $17,500. That's your half, and you know what, you're a great guy, and I appreciate your working with me. Here's an extra $500. Take your friend on a cruise and have a great time. Thanks so much for doing business with me." Did he expect that extra $500? No. Did it cost me? No, because I still made money, and it was still a good deal. Now, the next time I call Michael with a good deal, he'll likely be eager to partner with me.

I've wholesaled more than 200 properties in the past three years, 80 percent of them to one person. You can flip a house to someone once and make $12,000, or you can flip a similar house for a $9,000 profit to a person who's likely to buy five from you every year for the next 20 years. Whom do you work with? Do the math, and you'll answer that question for yourself.

Sometimes I borrow what's called *hard money* at high interest rates, and I'm glad to do it. For example, if Ina lends me hard money at 15 percent interest and 5 points, and I sell the property and make $20,000, I might give her an extra $100 to $200 to buy a nice dinner as my treat, even though I've paid her $5,000 to $8,000 in points. I thank her for doing the loan and tell her she's great. I know that when I call her next month, she'll want to work with me again.

Treat all of your customers like that all the time. Make a list of two or three extra things you can do for your customers, clients, or partners. And be sure to do those things! This will help your business and your long-term profitability. And it will make you happy.

Mistake # 5

Not Having a Written Plan for Your Investment Business

You've likely heard about the study of Harvard and Yale graduate students: Over the course of 30 years, 3 percent of the students in the study financially outperformed the other 97 percent because they had written plans and goals. It shows how rarely people write down their plans. Plans made only from good intentions sound like this: "I'm going to get some real estate, and something good will happen."

I encourage you to have a plan for every property. In fact, for every type of transaction, it's best to develop Plan A, Plan B, and Plan C. Focus on the activities that will get you to the goals stated in all three plan alternatives. If you want to make $8 million in real estate over the next seven years, that's possible if you're willing to work hard enough. (I offer a CD that has personality profiles, time profiles, and credit profiles that help you determine your plan. It's available at www.sheminrealestate.com)

Mistake # 6

Expecting to Have Equal Partnerships in Your Real Estate Investment Deals

Keep control of your business and realize that there's no such thing as an equal partnership.

I like this saying, which I think came from Confucius: "Happy wife makes happy husband." Here's an example of this. As I mentioned in the introduction, one of the investors who got me started was more than 70 years old when I met him. He'd married when he was 16, so he'd been wed to the same woman for almost 60 years. He and his wife still hold hands and love to kiss and hug. At the time I met them, I was engaged to be married, and I asked him his secret for staying married so long. He said, "Son, it's very simple. I'm going to give you some very profound advice.

"Before we got married, my wife came to me and said, 'Look, you're the man of the house. If there are any big decisions to be made, you're the man, so you make them, and I'll stand by you 100 percent. We have a partnership, and you're in charge of that area. I'm the woman of the house. If there are any little decisions, I'll make them, and whatever I decide, you stick by me.'

"Son, after 60 years, there hasn't been one big decision to make yet."

My point is that there's no equal partnership. Someone has to be in control of *your* business and it should be you.

Mistake # 7

Being Frightened to Do Large Deals

Suppose I've got a building for sale that's worth $5 million, and you can buy it from me for $3 million. Would you put a contract on it? Does it feel too big for you? But think about it: What's the difference between a $500,000 deal and a $5,000,000 deal? Only one zero. What difference does a zero make? Nothing.

I'm not telling you to go out and do bigger deals right now. You'll go hungry if you try that too soon. You've got to find your niche, your bread and butter, the place where you're comfortable. But I challenge you to open your mind, because when you look for motivated sellers, eventually you'll find someone who owns not one house, but 15. You'll find people who own apartment buildings or a commercial center as well as the house you're interested in. When they say they've got one available for sale, instead of being frightened about moving on it, put it under contract with your contingency, and then find a buyer. If it's a good deal, the right buyer will come along.

In bigger deals, the buyers are usually easier to deal with than in those small retail transactions. In this hypothetical example, when I try to sell my $60,000 home in Nashville to Billy Bob, I have to help him pay off his car, sell his wheelbarrow, and get a gift from his uncle so he can come up with a down payment. He's been divorced seven times and his fifth wife didn't sign the release form, so I have to chase her down to close the deal. In contrast, a commercial buyer asks for the numbers, goes to closing in 45 days, and has the bank wire the money immediately. The deal is complete.

Bill, a student who has become one of my best friends, came to my seminar years ago and told me, "Robert, you think too small." At the time, I was happy doing my little houses, and I thought my approach was working well for me, but he definitely wanted to make more money than I was making. He'd find plots of land, write to the owners, and put the land under contract, then go to developers and ask what they would pay for it. On the first deal that he flipped, he made $650,000. One year, Bill even called me about a university he had under contract and asked if I wanted to buy it.

Recently, one of the most successful entrepreneurs in Nashville died, leaving an estate of hundreds of millions of dollars. Bill did something no one else bothered to do (including myself, and I teach these things). About two weeks after this entrepreneur died, Bill called his widow and said, "I'm Bill. I knew your late husband. I know your son. I'm very sorry to hear about what happened. I know you have some real estate—would you like to get rid of it?" She said, "Thank God you called." She hated dealing with real estate and disliked the stress it had caused her husband. She owned 12 apartment buildings and 30 houses, and Bill put them all under contract for 60 cents on the dollar, then wholesaled them and made a ridiculous amount of money.

Bill also asked her the key question that you should to ask from now on: "Do you have anything else?" She said yes and invited him to follow her to the barn. Her husband collected antique cars and had 30 of them— Corvettes from the 1950s, Packards, woodies, and more. She said, "Please, can you help me out? I don't know what to do with these." Bill gladly put all of them under contract for $50,000. She was happy to get rid of them; she didn't need the money. And Bill sold the first car of the 30 for more than $50,000—what he'd paid for all of them.

Mistake # 8

Being Unclear Whether You Want
to Sell or Rent a Property

Owning rental property can be the best wealth builder around, but you need to decide whether you want to sell it and make the big cash, or rent it and build wealth slowly. If you want to sell, sell it; if you want to rent, rent it. Be decisive. Time is money.

I have fashioned my business on Chinese restaurants that can make money selling $1.50 egg rolls because of volume. I'm into volume and speed. Why? Because, like you, I only have one asset—and that's time.

To save time when selling a property, make this your policy and procedure: Set up automated systems, have prospective buyers drive by the property, and preapprove buyers over the phone.

Mistake # 9

Letting Your Business Get Out of Your Control and Run You

Bookkeeping, making phone calls, and dealing with tenants and potential buyers can keep you busy and stressed out. Remember, most investors get into real estate for one big reason—*freedom*. The rewards can be awesome, the wealth incredible, the vacations glorious. Frequently, I'm able to take two or three months off and go to Costa Rica and relax. But when you first get into real estate, you may become obsessed like I did, working all the time—7 A.M. to 11 P.M. If the phone rang at 10 at night, I'd answer it. If it rang on Saturday afternoon, I'd answer it. On Sunday, I'd go out and look at more property. I wanted to start a new group called REA, Real Estate Anonymous: "Hi, my name's Robert. I can't stop doing deals."

Real estate investing is fun, and you can make a lot of money, but don't do it all the time. Your family life, your personal life, and your spiritual life will suffer—and here's the weirdest part: You'll make less money. So even if you're a part-time investor, set office hours for yourself.

In my office, we don't take phone calls after 5 P.M. We have a separate phone line to deal with calls about repairs. And you know what? I've never missed a deal because I didn't answer the phone at 9:30 at night. People leave a voice mail; we call them back the next business day. In my experience, there simply haven't been any emergencies.

There's also a tendency in real estate to do everything yourself. I suggest you confine your activities to acquiring property, finding deals and putting

them together, because that's where you make your money. Don't spend time doing paperwork, dealing with tenants, managing, handling accounting and legal work—activities that give you headaches and don't make you any money. It's better to hire professionals and let them do their jobs. I did almost everything myself in the beginning, but as soon I could, I got a good title lawyer and bookkeeper. These people are essential.

Track how you spend your time and what makes money for you. My organization has a system for that. (Go to www.sheminrealestate.com for details.) Learn the system, because it will save you a lot of time and money.

My job now is to do next to nothing. I've got 45 people looking for deals for me. I have a bookkeeper who pays all my bills, both personal and business. I believe that everyone has a gift. Spending time exercising your gift makes you happy, and you'll have fun and make more money. And all the time you spend *not* exercising your gift could make you frustrated and stressed out. Chances are you'll make less money, too. So find out what you like to do and what you're good at, then let others handle the activities that support your talents.

No

You're ru
continually
educate yo
association
meeting wit

**After you g
determine
didn't spenc
But now I b
more money.
can get one ic
To find out a
that I am offe
call today. Sor
upcoming even**

Mistake # 11

Failing to Review You
and Overall Activit

Most businesses get into t

- *No cash flow.*
  this month

- *Bad acc*
  only

you about

rouble because of these problems:

Deals are about to close, but you can't pay the rent

ounting. In a lucrative year, you owe the IRS $30,000 but
have $18 left in your business bank account.

Poor management. Your management plan, if you have one, is
chaotic.

> The first year I learned to wholesale properties, I made 52 deals. I made a lot of money wholesaling houses; I had a lot of rentals that brought in $5,000 to $8,000 a week. Multiply that by 52 weeks (that's $260,000 to $416,000), and at the end of that year I said, "That worked great. Now I'm going to do something else." I went into managing property, because I'm good at it. I managed other people's properties. I had an office and a staff, and I gained status in the community. I felt important because everyone wanted to talk to me all the time. My employees and I were extremely busy and stressed out, but we made no money. We were collecting our rents and others' rents and doing rehabs and making wholesale deals. A lot of money came in, and a lot of money went out, but overall, it was a financial mess, because we'd take money from "here" to pay "there." One of the happiest days of my life was the day I sold my property management company. And here's the interesting part: When I got rid of a lot of my overhead, my profits skyrocketed.

Ever since that stressful time, I've vowed that every Friday, whatever business I'm in, I'll study a report of what's come in and what's gone out and what activities have taken place during the week. Now I get a report from the management company I hired and review the numbers without fail every Friday.

You see, if I only reviewed the numbers every month or two, I'd lose track of what's going on. I know that if something got out of control during the week, it could be radically out of control for the month. Most people actually wait a whole year before reviewing the numbers. Imagine the possibilities if things stayed out of control for an entire year! That's why it's best to identify problems early and frequently. Then you can lessen the amount of time that anything is in chaos.

I also sit down for 30 minutes each Friday and analyze how I spent my time during that week so as to determine what made me money and what didn't. (In my courses, I provide a simple worksheet to help with this task. It's actually best to fill it out every day, but at least do it once a week.)

In addition to tracking your time, I recommend that you project the amounts that will come in and go out, then determine what you'll need in the near future. If you can't do this calculation yourself, get someone who can. Hire a bookkeeper to scrutinize the numbers weekly. Yes, you will get ripped off and lose money from time to time. But if you see the books every week, you'll *know* it. If you let it go for months, it may become too late to turn around a chaotic situation.

Mistake # 12

Thinking That Real Estate Is Risky

Many people in real estate investing, especially beginners, think investing in real estate is risky. It certainly can be. However, real estate investing can be managed with almost zero risk if you get proper information and act on it.

Just like driving a car, riding a bicycle, or anything else in life, with the proper information, practice, skill, and procedures, your risk is greatly reduced. For example, in the past few months, I have been interviewed by reporters from many newspapers, magazines, and radio stations about the risky real estate market. Is the bubble bursting? Is it all too speculative to get into real estate right now? I reply that I'm wholesaling properties, so my risk (and yours, too, if you do it properly) is limited to only the time I invest in a property. Say you find a property worth $450,000 for $350,000 and wholesale it (line up a buyer) for $85,000 before you have to close on that property. You would make $35,000 on this deal. If you find a good deal, use proper disclosures that say you'll be reselling the property, then you're out of it before you are ever in it. The risk you take lies in *not* receiving and working with the proper information. You have to verify that the property really is worth $450,000 or more to get a good deal. Take time to gather comparable sales data and verify it with a strong, trustworthy market player to learn the real value of the property.

Think about any activity you do—any business you are in—and think about how having the right information limits your risk. How do you acquire the information you need?

- Try and fail; try and fail and learn (as I did).
- Learn from others; get a mentor (recommendations available by calling my office, 888-302-8018).
- Study, read, and attend classes at every stage of your business.
- Apply, experience, and improve—analyzing what works for you every step of the way.

If you get stuck on any deal or believe that the risk is too great, ask yourself: What information can you get that will reduce your risk? Whom can you call to get that information? Searching out the answers to these questions will greatly reduce your risk when making real estate buys.

Mistake # 13

Not Creating an Exit Strategy for Your Real Estate Business

It's easier to get *into* real estate than to get *out* of it. A real estate investing business plan for most people goes like this: "I'm going to get some property, and something good is going to happen." Thirty years later, they have 38 rental properties. Managing them is driving them nuts, and they want to retire. They can't sell them, because they'd have to pay too much in taxes. Their kids don't want to own or operate the properties, and they simply don't know what to do because they didn't put an exit strategy in place.

Every time you buy a property, write down your plan for it, and keep that plan in that property's file folder. For example, my Plan A for one house worth $120,000 is to wholesale it. I buy it for $80,000 and flip it to someone for $90,000, so I'll make $10,000. Plan B: If I can't wholesale it quickly enough, I'll find a hard moneylender who'll lend me the $80,000 to buy it. Then I'll have more time to sell it, because I know I can make money on it. Plan C: If I can't wholesale it or borrow hard money, I have a friend with great credit who wants to get into real estate. I've already talked with him and verified everything in writing. He'll borrow the money using his credit; we'll buy the home together and rent it out as 50-50 partners. Plan D: I have included a contingency clause in the contract; therefore, if nothing works out, I'll just back out.

You should have at least three or four exit strategies for every property—even for your rental properties. Know how you're going to get out of them. Are you going to sell them to tenants or another investor? Are you going to do a tax-free 1031 exchange? The point is that you need an exit strategy. Real estate is easier to get into than you think, but it can be difficult to get out of.

An exit strategy matters even if you think a deal is really bad. Let me tell you about one of the worst deals I ever made. I bought five duplexes for $18,000 and planned to spend $18,000 to fix them, which means I'd invest a total of $36,000 in them. I determined they'd be worth about $60,000 in the marketplace. I wanted to wholesale them, so I put them under contract. Unfortunately, these duplexes were in a really bad neighborhood. Even though they were appraised for $60,000, no one would buy them because of the part of town they were in. I thought I was stuck with them as rentals, so I borrowed money to fix them. (They really needed a lot of work—trash everywhere. I almost cried.) After I fixed them, I rented them fairly quickly and sold them a while later for $95,000.

Sometimes the deal just doesn't work. But even if you do a bad deal in real estate, time will cure it unless you're in a negative cash-flow situation and can't hang in there. If you *can* hang in there long enough, you'll likely come out ahead over time. In 1986, there was a nationwide real estate depression after the tax laws changed, and real estate values plummeted 30 to 40 percent. Yet most investors who hung on to their properties have seen their real estate values double, triple, or quadruple since 1986.

Mistake # 14

Wasting Time on Activities That Don't Make You Any Money and Simply Aren't Any Fun

For the next 90 days, take five minutes each morning to write a goal sheet for that day. Record the number of phone calls you're going to make, the number of properties you're going to look at, and the number of offers you're going to submit. Include whatever you think are good moneymaking and fun goals. Then, at the end of the day, spend five minutes to review your list. Notice what you accomplished and how much time you spent on each activity. Doing these two things will dramatically increase your happiness and your wealth.

On your daily call sheet, write this down every morning: "I am the Chief Executive Officer." You're the boss. And at the end of the day, ask yourself: Based on today's progress, would you hire, keep, or fire yourself? If you were paying yourself as an employee, how would you rate yourself on your activity? I would have fired myself almost every week, because I was spending my time shuffling papers on my desk, calling friends, eating lunch, and reading books, but not taking action.

Most of us find something that makes us a lot of money, then we don't do it again. What made you a lot of money in the last year or two? How did you find your deals? Now decide to do more of what brought you those deals. If someone helped you find a good deal, talk to that person every few weeks. Check to see if there are any more.

Be honest with yourself. If you're like most people, you'll find you're spending only 10 percent of your time doing things that will make you money.

Mistake # 15

Not Having the Right Insurance to Properly Cover Your Investments

Investing in real estate can be risky, and you might encounter legal problems along the way. I challenge you to write down all of the activities you're involved in: looking for houses, buying houses, managing properties, doing repairs, and so on. Then ask your insurance broker, "Am I covered by my insurance for all these activities?" The answer is probably no. You have car insurance—but remember, if you put people in your car to show them real estate, you are involved in a commercial activity that might not be covered under your regular insurance. Be sure to check. If you do repairs yourself on your own rental homes and someone gets injured or killed in your home, you could be sued. Your property and fire insurance carriers might refuse to pay a claim because you don't have a contractor's or builder's insurance policy. They'll say you're not covered. Make sure you're properly insured for all the activities you're involved in.

My friend was rehabbing a house and helped the contractor by delivering materials for the deck and holding the wood. The deck was designed to hold 15 people. Shortly after moving in, the buyers hosted a party. About 30 people stood on the deck, and it collapsed. A lot of them went to the hospital in an ambulance. (In law school, I learned that if you ever get in an accident, always go to the hospital in an ambulance—you're likely to receive a bigger settlement.) The contractor was sued for millions of dollars and went bankrupt. My friend's insurance company told him he was acting as a contractor and had no contractor's insurance to protect that activity. Fortunately, he had set up proper asset protection through limited liability companies and land trusts. He was able to settle all claims for a few thousand dollars instead of hundreds of thousands of dollars because they couldn't access his assets. Don't let that happen to you. Make sure you have proper insurance.

Mistake # 16

Being Underinsured on Your Auto Insurance Coverage

I want to protect you from facing a big lawsuit. Go to your insurance broker and find out how much car insurance you have. Most of us have $300,000 to $400,000 in coverage, but if you caused a car accident and a child died or an adult couldn't work for 20 years, how much would the judgment or settlement be? Probably much more than your coverage—$400,000 can disappear fast when you're paying for intensive care treatments or covering a settlement.

You're far more likely to be sued for a car accident than for a real estate deal, and you could face a crippling lawsuit. For homework, call your auto insurance broker and ask about the size of the judgments being awarded where you live. Then ask if you have enough insurance, and get the answer in writing. If your broker says $200,000 is plenty and tells you not to worry about it, and you or your teenager then gets sued for a judgment of $800,000 two years later, your insurance broker committed errors and omissions and could be held responsible in court.

When I was 16, I was dismissed from high school with the rest of my class to see President Carter speak. But that day, just about everyone went to a big party at a waterfall instead of seeing President Carter. We did no drinking or drugs at this gathering. Driving our family's station wagon back home, I had to go on a broken-up road where about 20 people had been killed over the years. I wasn't speeding, but I accidentally flipped the station wagon off the side of a mountain, and some friends in the car were badly hurt. Thank God, everybody is okay now. But I spent three years, from ages 16 to 19, involved in two major lawsuits with some of my best friends (which we settled). One of my friends was in intensive care for two weeks and in hospital care for a month; his medical bills totaled $880,000. (Imagine what that would cost today.)

Six weeks before this accident happened, my father had purchased an umbrella insurance policy. He was the first person in Nashville to buy a $1 million umbrella policy. It cost him $120. (They cost about $200 a year now.) That policy covered all the costs from this accident. If he hadn't purchased it, where would my family be today? Where would you be if something like that happened?

Find out how much an umbrella policy costs, and get enough to cover your properties, too. Most people have the standard $200,000 or $300,000 in coverage. If there is a house fire and someone gets killed or badly burned and is hospitalized, settlements would cost a lot more.

Say you own a house on Jones Street and have a $500,000 insurance policy on both yourself and the house. Then you transfer the title of the house to a land trust. A fire breaks out in that house, and someone sues both the land trust and you—and wins a judgment. Your insurance broker will say you don't own the house anymore; it's owned by a trust. Consequently, the complainant can't collect.

So when you transfer your properties to limited liability companies (LLCs), land trusts, or limited partnerships, make sure the insurance policy names the entity as the insured. On my insurance, I have named about 15 insureds, because I always get mixed up about which entity I'm using, so I just write down all my LLCs and land trusts. The insurance company doesn't care as long as an insurable interest is named in the paperwork.

Mistake # 17

Not Taking Advantage of Affordable Legal Services

I'm an attorney by training. I'm also an independent associate with Pre-Paid Legal Services. I have used this service for five years and have been involved with them as a side business for three years. I sell Pre-Paid Legal Services as an employee benefit to small and medium-sized companies around the country. I think it's the hottest employee benefit going and should be considered by every employer.

The American Bar Association (ABA), which most of the judges and lawyers in the United States belong to, has looked at Pre-Paid Legal Services. In many published articles about Pre-Paid Legal, the ABA is quoted as saying, "Americans have come to view the legal system as a necessity. The best way for the majority of Americans to be able to assure themselves of legal assistance when they need it is through a pre-paid legal plan." They didn't say a "pretty good" way, or a "kind of good" way—they said the *best* way.

**   *Forbes, Fortune, USA Today*, and the *Wall Street Journal* are all recommending Pre-Paid Legal Services. Every year, *Forbes* ranks the 200 best small and medium-sized companies in the United States. Pre-Paid Legal has been in the top 15 for the past five years in a row. It has been ranked as the thirty-third fastest growing company on the New York Stock Exchange.**

**   Are you worried about getting sued? You should be. You have a three times greater chance of being named in a legal action and going to court than you do of going to the hospital. And that statistic is about five years old. Chances are you have health insurance to cover health-related expenses. Where's your legal insurance?**

The basic membership for Pre-Paid Legal is $26 a month. Your auto and health insurance rates have probably increased in the past five years, but Pre-Paid Legal's rates are not likely to change. The contract is month to month, so you can sign up, try it out, and cancel if you don't like it. However, I recommend that you keep it for at least a year to get some benefit from it.

Who's covered? You, your spouse, your children through college age (23 if they're still in school). You're covered throughout the entire United States. Pre-Paid Legal Services has 100,000 top attorneys in its system, using only the best attorneys in each state. That's how the service gets such good ratings.

Have you ever been overcharged for house or car repairs? You should have called Pre-Paid Legal. Ever had difficulty returning a product or service? You should have let your lawyer handle that. Ever gotten a traffic ticket? Pre-Paid Legal would have gone to court for you. Ever not gotten a security deposit back? Been audited? Bought a home, signed a contract, made a will? You need Pre-Paid Legal.

The service covers almost any legal need you could have in the areas of bankruptcy, criminal law, and real estate law. As a real estate investor, you'll have legal questions, so make it easy to get answers.

Pre-Paid Legal has been around for 30 years. It's a good company offering a product that works for a good value. Its coverage includes the following items:

- *Phone calls about legal issues.* Unlimited phone calls for personal or business questions. Lawyers usually charge $200 to $300 an hour. Most legal issues are dealt with through phone consultations.
- *Letters.* If you have a case against someone, let the law firm write a letter with 50 lawyers' names across the top of it. "Take it off the credit report." "Insurance company, do the right thing." "Fix the car." "Contractor, finish the paint job." Without Pre-Paid Legal, it would cost $200 to $300 to have an attorney write a letter.

- *Contract review.*   Use this service any time you sign a contract—house purchase, car purchase, loan, cell phone agreement, private school agreement, employment agreement, and so on. Wealthy, smart families get their attorneys to look at all contracts before they sign them. Recently I bought a car and sent the contract to be reviewed by a Pre-Paid Legal lawyer. I'm a lawyer myself, and the contract looked good to me. However, he found that the contract showed a $400 destination charge for a used car! How many contracts will you sign when you don't know exactly what you're signing?
- *Wills.*   Everyone needs a will. An estate-planning attorney charges $200 to $800 to draw up a will. I'm on a mission to get everyone to have their wills written, and Pre-Paid Legal Services is my ally in this. A friend of mine heard a presentation about this a few years ago and decided to think about the service before signing up. I told him, "It's only $26 a month. Sign up and get your will done. You have kids. Then if you don't like Pre-Paid after you get your will done, just cancel it." Seven weeks after that conversation, while he was still thinking about it, he and his wife were driving around Nashville and had to stop at a red light. A drunk driver ran the light, crashed into their car, and killed them both instantly. Because they didn't have a will that named a guardian, both of their children went into state custody. The children's grandparents spent four months fighting the courts before they could get the children released. In fact, one of my friends claims to have filed a will just so certain people in the family *won't* get custody of the kids if anything happens! So please make your will. To get started, go to www.prepaidlegal.com/info/shemin to find out about Pre-Paid Legal, or call my office, 888-302-8018.

Almost everyone has a hole in his or her insurance coverage. If you cause a bad car accident and someone dies as a result, you will be charged with involuntary manslaughter or vehicular homicide. Your car insurance will pay for medical bills and damage to your car, but it won't pay for criminal defense. Pre-Paid Legal Services was founded for this reason. Its lawyers will defend you if you're charged with vehicular homicide or manslaughter.

If you are sued, Pre-Paid Legal provides 75 hours a year of time from top attorneys to defend you. That's about $15,000 to $20,000 in the bank—enough to cover your defense for most of what you're involved in. If you are audited, Pre-Paid Legal provides up to 50 hours of tax attorney time. These are lawyers, not accountants. You can call and ask any legal tax question. (Don't use accountants to deal with the IRS; they don't have to follow confidentiality rules as attorneys do.)

Instead of paying a high hourly rate for other legal work that may not be covered by Pre-Paid Legal, you get a discount rate of $150 an hour. For instance, if you have to sue someone, Pre-Paid Legal covers phone calls and letters, but if you have to go to court, you'd be charged at the discounted rate.

Pre-Paid Legal Services also provides a form of legal shield. If the police pull you over to question or detain you for a criminal matter, just being able to call your attorney seven days a week, 24 hours a day can help the situation.

Mistake # 18

Not Developing a Long-Term Plan to Protect Your Real Estate Assets

Everyone has different risks. Before you develop a plan, you need to determine what both your assets and your risks are. If you own apartment buildings and hotels, for example, your asset protection needs are different from those of someone who owns three houses. What is the real risk? Find out what the largest judgments awarded against people that do your business in your area have been. You can't protect against what you don't know. In most states, it's difficult to find a judgment against a small property owner for over $500,000, so the first question is what are you protecting yourself *against?* To set up a plan, get advice from your attorney and insurance broker.

Who are the people who sue other people? Upset and angry people. Therefore, here's the best policy and procedure you can ever adopt: Don't make people angry.

A management company about the same size as the one I use gets sued 10 times a year. The people who work there upset people constantly. They don't return phone calls, they don't do repairs, they yell at the tenants, and more. My management company works hard to keep its tenants and avoid being sued.

If all of your assets are in your name and you get sued, the winner of the suit can conceivably be awarded everything you own. I suggest transferring some or all of your assets out of your own name. Anonymity does not always protect your assets, but it certainly helps.

I suggest setting up land trusts for anonymity, because it's harder for plaintiffs to find you. However, a good attorney would hire a good private investigator to do a nationwide search and find your assets, even if you had them in LLCs and land trusts. Attorneys can also get a judge to order you to disclose where your assets are in some situations.

Did you know that the Marriott and Hyatt hotel corporations own their real estate in LLCs, not land trusts? If an LLC is good enough for them with their $10 million buildings, it's good enough for you and me with our $100,000 rental houses.

Check with your attorney whether it's better to have an LLC or a land trust. There are some tax requirements in some states with certain LLCs—franchise and excise tax. But 95 percent of attorneys and accountants who handle real estate suggest putting the property you own in a corporation—a limited liability company.

The best asset protection tools are retirement accounts—401(k)s, self-directed pension plans, and Individual Retirement Accounts (IRAs). It's difficult for someone who wants to sue you to get at your pension plan through the courts.

Another asset protection tool is life insurance. Florida and Texas have homestead laws that offer protection for your principal residence. During one of the largest bankruptcies in Tennessee, for example, the people in bankruptcy bought an $18 million house in Florida for cash and kept it.

Any time you attempt asset protection, you could encounter problems with your lenders and face questions about estate planning and taxes. A lot of banks don't want you to put assets into LLCs, so many investors take out a bank loan in their name and then quitclaim it into an LLC, understanding that they could be violating the "due on sale" clause. Other investors get permission from the bank to do that.

However, your first line of defense against a judgment is insurance. I keep some properties in my own name because I'm always buying, selling, and refinancing, and don't have time to move them in and out of LLCs and land trusts. I also keep a lot of insurance to protect my assets.

Mistake # 19

Setting Up an Asset Protection Plan Improperly

Are you concerned that someone will slip and fall or have another kind of accident on your property? Don't worry; you most likely have insurance to cover that. But big investors really worry about dealing with big accidents and million-dollar lawsuits that can strip them of their assets. They want to protect those assets, yet they have to avoid stating that as a purpose. Here's a solution. Ask for a free asset protection consultation today by calling 888-302-8018. An attorney will consult with you in absolute confidentiality for free—a $100 value. Leave your name, address and phone number, and an asset protection specialist will call you back.

As in any profession, there are good attorneys and bad attorneys. It's the really good ones I'm worried about. In fact, I learned what I know about asset protection from good attorneys who build strong cases and sue people for a living.

You could attend an asset protection course and learn how to set up an LLC and a land trust, then put all of your assets in them and assume that no one can access them through a lawsuit. But a good lawyer could charge you with fraudulent conveyance for doing that.

Here's example of what could happen. Jeff is a landlord who put his rental property in trusts. Victor and his family are his tenants. The electrical wiring on the property had been installed improperly and caused a fire. Sadly, Victor and his family got burned in the fire. Millions of dollars in lawsuits followed. A good lawyer would ask Jeff why he put his property into this land trust and LLC. The lawyer would propose to the jury that the only reason Jeff did so was to protect himself and keep the tenants from getting their fair due. But is what he did fair? Victor and his lawyer will charge Jeffrey with fraudulent conveyance, asserting that he set up a trust specifically to defraud the tenants from getting their fair due. There are two conditions attached to fraudulent conveyance. First, Jeff had to do it with the intent of defrauding his clients. Second, his finances had to be insolvent when he transferred his assets to his LCC and land trust. Most people set up LLCs and trusts (forms of asset protection) when it's too late. You can avoid that by first putting together a financial statement that shows you're solvent, signing and dating it, and putting it in your file. (You can get the right form at the bank or from my course.) Basically, this form shows that you make more than you owe.

Then, if you're going to set up LLCs and land trusts, have your attorney or accountant write a letter saying it's good estate planning to do so. In real estate circles, you present a good image when you put your properties in an LLC. A land trust will give you some estate planning edge, too. Be sure you have that letter in your file, so that if you're ever taken to court, you can produce a document stating that you set the LLC and land trust up for estate planning reasons. In court, the opposing attorney will likely ask, "Did you set up the LCC and trust for asset protection?" You can respond by saying, "Well, it has some of those benefits, but I have the reason right here in writing, dated years ago." Never mention the term *asset protection*.

Mistake # 20

Missing Out on Special Loan Programs

If you buy, fix up, and sell or rent in low- to moderate-income areas, look into the special loan programs available. At certain times of the year they're funded; at other times, they're not. You want to catch them at the end of their fiscal year, which for most companies is December 31. They might be in a frenzy to spend the rest of their money for that year. Take advantage of their programs.

Three special loan programs are available:

- *Rental Rehab Program.* This locally administered program will match or grant the repair money if you buy and fix up a property and rent or sell it to low-income tenants.
- *Community Reinvestment Act.* The federal government and federally chartered banks are under pressure to lend funds to people in low- to moderate-income neighborhoods. Visit your bank and ask if a property you're considering qualifies for this assistance.
- *Emergency Weatherization.* The Department of Energy funds local and state housing authorities to insulate and weatherize properties rented to low- to moderate-income tenants and eligible elderly people. When a tenant applies for the funds, a government representative comes out to do an analysis. My office offers a program in which we help our tenants apply for this benefit. We have the applications, we help them fill it out, and we make sure the proper authorities get involved. The program helps landlords maintain their properties, too. One year, the government spent $60,000 insulating and weatherizing some of my properties, and the work included putting in new windows and doors.

Mistake # 21

Running Out of Cash and the Bills Keep Coming

A few years ago, tornadoes hit 150 of my properties, and 30 of them were almost destroyed. I had $180,000 in rent due to come in; $90,000 in notes, taxes, and insurance going out; and $270,000 cash in my operating account. I also knew I could go for a while without collecting any rent and still pay all my bills. But about seven weeks after the disaster, I ran out of cash and tapped into all my credit lines and credit cards. Running out of money can be the worst feeling in the world. The breaking point for me came on a Saturday afternoon when my nine-year-old son wanted to go to a movie, and I didn't have enough money to take him—I had no cash. I sat in my office and cried. I felt too embarrassed to call my family and ask for help. Then I got an idea. I looked in the closet and found a jar filled with coins, then went to the grocery store and cashed them in. I found a total of $88.53 and it seemed like $1 million. With that money, I was able to take my son out to the movies on Saturday and take my family out to dinner on Sunday. On Monday, the bank floated me an emergency loan, which got me out of the crisis.

Based on this experience, here's what I'd do differently. I would hire a professional insurance adjuster or an attorney who understands what to do in case of a fire, flood, tornado, or other emergency. Once I found a good adjuster to work with, I would immediately triple the amount of the insurance claim on the damage to my properties.

Second, I would make sure I put 10 percent of everything I earned into savings. If you save $89 a week for 30 years and can make 11 percent interest on it, you'll have more than $1 million. If you learn to do creative financing, you might even be able to make more than that. Say you put away $89 a week at 18 percent. You'll have more than $5 million after 30 years. Start saving now to cover yourself in case of an emergency. Doing it faithfully will change your life.

Mistake # 22

Not Having the Proper Team in Place

People on your team make the difference between having an okay business and a great business. Most real estate investors are independent; they like to do everything themselves and don't want to deal with other people. They want to close the deals, do the paperwork, manage the property, and take care of the repairs—because the only person they trust is themselves. However, if you have the proper team in place, you'll be able to solve any question or problem you have, instantly—and be able to make more money.

As a real estate investor, I recommend that you build a team that includes these professionals:

- *Real estate attorney or title lawyer.* This person handles all details for the closings and understands wholesaling, lease options, and contracts. (Don't go to your family lawyer and say you want to do creative real estate deals. Go to a specialist in this field.)
- *Contractor and repair people.* Be in contact with two to five of them. Make sure they're referred, licensed, bonded, and insured. Use a contractor instead of a property inspector, because a contractor can tell you how much it would cost to fix something, not just that it's in need of repair.
- *Mortgage brokers.* They acquire mortgages for you and for buyers of your properties. Work with them to get buyers preapproved for mortgages.
- *Appraisers.* They tell you what properties are worth.
- *Certified Public Accountants (CPAs).* They handle your paperwork. (I prefer to work with CPAs who own real estate themselves, because they keep on top of the new tax laws, write-offs, and depreciations.)

- *Real estate agents.* They help you retail your properties and get information on the value of comparable properties (comps).
- *Other real estate investors.* They are your best source of information, pricing, and referrals. Meet with two or three investors a week. Talk with them on the phone. Take one to lunch every week. Through them, I've learned a lot about real estate, and I've also gotten deals that way.
- *Property manager.* This person helps to verify rents before you wholesale to landlords.

Many people hesitate to deal in real estate because certain questions hold them back. For example, you're not sure how to wholesale a property or do the paperwork, so you think you'd better not do it at all. You don't put a property under contract because you're not sure what it's worth. You want to wholesale a property, but you might have to pay a lot of taxes, so you decide to not do anything until you find out about that. Consequently, you just wait around. Isn't that what's keeping you from doing this business—the questions you have?

When you have lined up your team of professionals, any question that holds you up from doing a deal can be fixed using Robert's Rule of 7 or 10, that is: What 7 or 10 numbers can you dial to get answers? If you have a contract problem, call your title person. If you have an accounting problem, call your accountant. If you have a question about comps, call your agent or appraiser. If you have a repair problem, call your contractor.

People ask me what I know about real estate. I tell them, nothing. I don't know what houses are worth. I've done about 600 transactions in Nashville and a couple of hundred within a four-mile radius of that city, but I still don't know what properties will be worth. Every time I think one is worth $150,000, my neighbors sell their house for $160,000. Every time I get a deal at 50 cents on the dollar, my buddy gets one at 40 cents on the dollar. Every time I rent out a property for $1,000 a month, the guy down the street rents a similar place for $1,200. The only people who know the answers are those who are active in the market every day, the professionals. So my question is this: Whose number should I call?

People love to do two things: Eat lunch and give free advice. One day, I was taking the most successful businessperson in my state out to lunch. I told him I was having trouble getting sources of funding for my real estate. He asked me if I'd like to learn how to borrow a couple of million dollars in 30 minutes. I thought he was kidding. In fact, the way he posed the question, I thought he was delivering an infomercial like the ones on television.

But this investor immediately called a bank president who didn't even know him. He said, "You don't know me, but I'm here with Robert, and he's a new real estate investor. He's got a very interesting business model. John, you're a well-respected businessperson in the community. We really look up to you. I know you're busy. [Notice how he's building rapport.] Look, we don't want to borrow any money from you. We'd like to come in for 15 to 20 minutes and get your advice about this business plan. Would you mind?" John agreed.

I had put together a business plan for buying and renting duplexes through Section 8 and helping people in low-income neighborhoods. I had a few photographs of my deals in my identity package (in my courses, you'll learn how to build these). John's defenses were down since we'd told him that I didn't want to borrow any money. I did say I was having problems getting financing and asked him for his ideas on how I could implement this plan, since it would greatly benefit the community (bankers are required to think about that these days). He picked up the phone and said to his receptionist, "Get the head of commercial lending in here, as well as the heads of private banking and residential mortgages. This is a great business plan." This bank lent me a lot of money as a result of getting in the door and showing him my business plan—and it all started with a networking lunch.

I suggest that you always seek the advice and experience of someone who's borrowed a lot of money. Find successful people and get them involved in your business.

Mistake # 23

Not Establishing Good Relationships with Those in the Investment Business and Service Providers

Take your time to find people who behave ethically and have a stellar reputation. You only want to refer others to team members whom you know do *good* business.

Any time you run into a roadblock, instead of worrying about it, all you have to do is pick up the phone and dial a few numbers to get the answer you need. For example, if you want to know what a piece of property is worth in a particular part of town, call your real estate agent friends and ask them to run comps. Similarly, if you have a problem with a contract or a title, call your title company representative or your closing agent to get the answer. They know all about those things. They're part of your support team and your overall system. Stop wondering, stop worrying; just call someone for help.

Mistake # 24

Getting Stuck with a Rehab House That Won't Sell or a Rental House That Won't Rent

Any time a property won't sell, there's usually one of two things going on: Either the price is wrong, or something is physically wrong. To fix the price problem, start thinking about the terms of sale rather than the price itself. When a property won't sell because it's physically wrong, there's usually a problem with its layout. Have confidence that you can overcome both of these obstacles.

Do you realize that half of all cars sold today are really leased, not purchased? Similarly, in real estate, you can often address the price problem by turning your property into a lease-option or rent-to-own situation. To address the layout problem, bring in a contractor or architect to offer suggestions, such as reconfiguring the kitchen or knocking out a wall to improve the traffic flow. Make sure you can afford to make the suggested changes. And have faith that you'll find the right solution for the situation.

Mistake # 25

Failing to Include a Contingency Clause When Putting Together a Contract

I recommend that you make sure your contract includes a contingency clause—a way out. It has always been known that information reduces your risk. Surgeons spend years getting information and developing their skills before they perform their first surgery. That knowledge and experience reduces their risk. Having correct information, knowledge, and experience reduces your risk in real estate, too. If you have a contingency clause, a way to get out, your risk is minimal. If you have a contingency clause and you have put in earnest money, make sure you get the earnest money back. When you do this properly, your financial risk is zero (other than the time and effort you put into it, which is worth more than the money to me).

In most situations, you only need one contingency clause that says: "This contract is contingent upon buyer's inspection and approval solely at the buyer's discretion. This contract is contingent upon the buyer receiving favorable financing, solely according to the buyer." The term "favorable financing" is left vague intentionally. There is some argument that this contingency clause is too broad and too open, so understand that if you engineer a giant commercial deal and get sued, and the case goes to the Supreme Court, this clause may not hold up. But it works for most people in most cases.

Alternatively, you can say "Contingent upon partner's inspection and approval." That's not too broad or open. Your partner can be a spouse, a real estate agent, an investment association leader, a horoscope reader—whatever. Because things change, you never want to sign a contract that doesn't have a contingency clause.

Mistake # 26

Not Negotiating with the Decision Maker Who Can Really Help You

When a sticky situation comes up, it's common for people to start out by dealing with others who can't make a decision about the issue at hand. For example, when patrons at a restaurant are served a bad meal, they yell at the waitress, when the manager is the person they need to talk to. Make a point of always first asking the person you're dealing with whether he or she can make the final decision—about the poor food or service, about the price of a television set, about the cost of the loan, about the price of the house, and so on.

My father would walk into a store and ask right off the bat, "Hey, where's the manager?" A manager would come over, and my father would take a moment to ask whether he was really the manager. "Yes I am," the man would reply.

"Great," my father would say, "but are you the manager in charge of this department?"

"No, that's the other manager," he would reply.

When the right manager was with him, my dad would ask, "This TV is going for $800, but there are a lot of deals out there, and I was looking to see if your store is ever going to have a sale or special on this TV. What can you do for me?" About 75 percent of the time, the department manager was able to give him a price reduction. Half the time, he also got other items thrown in. That's the power of negotiation.

I lead a seminar titled "You Can't Learn Anything in a Seminar." The premise is that you can come and get information, but you can't learn what you need to in the seminar itself; you only learn that when you apply it. That's the way of the world. I know you'll make mistakes when you start making real estate deals. Practice negotiating for what you want, just for fun, because it will help you negotiate bigger and better deals.

Here's some homework. The next time you go to a restaurant, ask the waiter to bring the manager over after your meal. He'll think that something bad happened and you're complaining, so reassure the waiter that everything is okay. When the manager comes over, express your delight with the meal and the staff. Compliment the service and food; be honest and sincere with your compliments. Tell the manager you just wanted to say thank you. That will make him or her feel good, because few people bother to do that. In the process of talking, you're doing something that's essential in negotiating—building rapport. In no time, that person will like you, because almost everyone else only complains.

While you've got the manager's attention, ask an open-ended question like this: "Do you ever do anything special for your customers?" In response, he or she might offer you a dessert, a discount, or a free drink. If you ask that question enough times in enough situations, you'll be certain to get something for your trouble. Try to negotiate for something every day—food, clothing, or electronics—by asking whether the restaurant or store ever runs a sale (or whatever makes sense in the situation). Even ask this question of your attorney, mortgage broker, accountant, and real estate agent. Ask them, "Are there any specials for regular customers? I might become one."

If you save 1 to 20 percent on every deal, what does that mean for you? Say that for every $2 you earn, you save $1. When you save that $1, you've effectively doubled your income because of its after-tax value: For example, if you put away $10,000, you've really saved $20,000 (depending on your tax bracket) because of the taxes that would apply.

Mistake # 27

Lamenting That Your Property Isn't Selling Fast Enough

What can you do to speed up the sale of your property? Use a buyers list. Do massive advertising. Reexamine how you're getting the word out. Put up a good sign. (About 60 percent of homes are still sold because the buyer saw a sign in the yard.) Use the Internet so that people who start to look at neighborhoods that way can find your houses. If your property isn't selling, beef up your marketing program.

It's estimated that 40 to 50 percent of all properties will be auctioned off over the next five years. If you conduct an auction to sell a property, you advertise it in the paper for 30 days. You hold the auction sale and the property closes within 20 days, so you get your money back quickly. At auctions, a lot of people generally show up, get excited, and bid too much compared to the worth of the property. At least once a year, I've auctioned some of my properties. Every time, I've received more than I thought I would and taken in way more than my minimum requirement for the property. I've also been able to build a big buyers list of the people who attend these auctions.

Mistake # 28

Making the Contract Process More Complicated Than It Has to Be

Putting together real estate contracts holds back 80 percent of my students. They hesitate because they feel unsure about how the paperwork needs to be completed. That's totally unnecessary. To get started, you can ask for a standard contract from your local real estate association and use the association's expertise to help you complete it.

Just to make this point loud and clear, I want to give you some extreme examples of how specific investors have simplified the contract process.

One of the most successful real estate investors in the United States lives in Florida and buys about 20 houses a month. When he negotiates with a motivated seller and gets a good deal, he writes on a piece of paper "I [the seller] hereby deed [the address of the property] to [buyer's name]," then he dates and signs it. At that point, the house belongs to him, even though his note hasn't been notarized or recorded yet, because the seller has just deeded it over. Then, for the down payment on the property, the investor writes an out-of-state check, which he knows will take seven days to clear. As soon as he leaves the house he just bought, he calls his title attorney and asks him to run the title records on that house. Sometimes a title search reveals tax liens or questionable ownership, so he needs to know that about his new property. If a problem turns up, he writes the seller a letter saying the contract is void. He cancels his check and renegotiates or moves on. If everything works out and the title is clear, he requires the seller go to the attorney and sign a real deed with a real closing statement. That's how simple he keeps his business—he literally works from one handwritten sheet of paper to put together a contract.

Human beings always love to complicate things. You can have the best contract in the world, but half the time sellers or real estate agents won't sign it because they want to use their own. Then they start fighting about paperwork.

I have my attorney write the contract because then he's on the hook. He has insurance for errors and omissions, and operates under a very high professional standard.

I recommend focusing on making money and helping people in real estate, not spending your time fighting over the wording of your contracts. I also try to get my clauses in there, but I don't always succeed, so I make a business decision and usually walk away from those deals.

As investors, our job is to find deals, put them together, and move on without getting hung up on the paperwork. I like to use a one-page standard buyer's contract, which is legal in every state and has all the disclaimers and disclosures in it. I use a one-page contract because I deal with motivated sellers who are already nervous and skittish. If I went in with an 80-page contract, I'd risk scaring them off, and they'd walk away from the deal altogether.

I also believe that if someone is going to rip me off, they'll willingly sign a 1,000-page contract written by the best attorney but still lie, cheat, and steal. Honest people keep agreements they've sealed on a handshake. (That being said, I always put my agreements in writing, and you should, too.) My father once told me, "A leopard doesn't change its spots." If certain people are dishonest, they're going to behave dishonestly, so stay away from them.

Mistake # 29

Negotiating a Good Cash Offer on an Attractive Piece of Property, but Leaving Money on the Table

The most money you'll ever make in real estate will come from negotiating. Are you ready to have some fun? You don't have to negotiate if you make enough low offers that are accepted. But imagine how much more you'd "win" if you knew how to negotiate.

The biggest mistake you can make when negotiating a deal of any kind is focusing on *yourself*: how much you'll offer, what your needs and goals are, and how you'll convince sellers to sell their homes to you. Instead of being so self-absorbed, focus on the person you're negotiating with. Remember, the number-one thing to look for in real estate is a motivated seller. How do you find out if a seller is motivated? By asking, "Why are you selling?" Never make assumptions; a lot of people who sell real estate don't need money, so selling property for a financial gain isn't always a prime motivator.

The first step in negotiating is to build rapport. Actually, people really learn to hone their negotiating skills while they're dating. Generally, when men try to impress women they want to date, they think about themselves rather than the women they're talking with. Here's another approach. A guy could weave a conversation with a new female acquaintance around an article he's just read about the three factors that are most important to women in relationships. He'd ask what those three things would be for *her*, and, by listening well, he'd learn what was really important in her life. He'd find out what her core values were, what she needed, wanted, and desired. By doing this, he'd be building rapport, not discussing a deal or making desperate demands on her.

The following principle stands true in any negotiation: The less you care about the outcome, the more you're likely to make. Desperation doesn't work. People are repelled by that kind of energy. If a man begs a woman for three digits of her phone number and declares he'll figure out the rest of the numbers, he comes across as desperate. Chances are, she won't be interested in him. In your real estate transactions, you might be doing the same thing—desperately begging for a deal. Instead, be natural. Take time to get to know the other negotiator and build rapport. It's not about you; it's about the other person.

Here's an example. When you call on a For Sale ad in the paper, start the conversation by asking the sellers questions about themselves first. What neighborhood do they live in? Do they like it? How long have they been living there? What brought them there? What kind of work to they do? How did they get into that line of work? How long have they been doing that? I spend 10 to 15 minutes asking others about themselves before the subject of the property ever comes up. I often let the sellers bring up the subject first. It's a big mistake to call and introduce yourself as a real estate investor, then immediately ask how much they want for their house. Build rapport first.

Second, understand the sellers' motivation. Remember that the number-one motivator for most people is fear of loss. It's possible that the sellers are afraid that if they don't deal with you, they'll lose their chance to sell their property. So institute fear, legally and ethically. And always be honest and upfront. Ask how long they've been in the house. Ask what the price is and how they came up with that number. Ask how soon they need to sell the house. Again, you're looking for signs of motivation. Ask why, why, why? If you don't have motivation, you don't have a deal.

Also ask what the debt is on the house so you know how much money they must have to cover that debt. People may not tell you this unless you've built rapport, but you can remind them that it's public knowledge; they don't have to tell you, you can get it from the public records (from the registrar of deeds or the tax broker).

Ask what's the absolute least amount they would take for the house if they could close in (whatever time frame they said). Then stay quiet and let them come up with a price. Ask this question at least three times.

Don't only negotiate on price—negotiate on *everything*, including terms, closing times, and closing costs. One of the biggest issues for people is terms—how and when funds will be paid.

Never ask for terms in so many words. Instead, ask what *they* want. Often people say they just have to get out of the loan, the bank is calling, they're moving out of state, they owe $80,000, and so on. In effect, they're asking for help, and that's what you want to do—help them. Say, "Great, we'll get you out of this house quickly. Will that solve your problem?" If you're going to pay cash, ask for a discount. Ask, "If you received the cash now instead of at the end of the term, what would you do with it?" If they need cash immediately, they'll likely accept less for the home.

People who are motivated don't care how you fix their problem; they just want it fixed. So build rapport and find out what the seller really needs, using ordinary language, not real estate lingo.

Mistake # 30

Not Verifying Everything with a Third Party

Think about all the times you've gotten frustrated or been ripped off. If you had verified a few more facts in the transaction, frustrating things likely wouldn't have happened. A lot of times, people don't purposely misrepresent prices and costs; they just aren't sure about them, or it's not their area of expertise.

A while ago, an investor sent me a deal on a house and included all the comps. This house comped out at $400,000; he had five comparable sales that were very recent and looked just like it. I looked at them. A real estate agent gave them to me; she swore they were accurate, and they probably were. Everything looked great.

But it's my policy always to verify information with a third party. David, a real estate agent in the area where this house is located, knows the market well. I called him for his opinion. (I always make sure that he gets paid for services like this over time.) He said they'd comp out at $400,000, but they'd take a long time to sell, which was critical information.

The lesson is that you always want written verification of information in your file. This pertains to repairs, too. If a contractor says the repairs will cost a certain amount, I get someone else to verify it.

Mistake # 31

Making Only One Offer on a Property Instead of Three

Every time you make an offer, the probability that it will be accepted is 50-50. If you make three offers on the same property, your odds of having your offer accepted triple. After you negotiate and find out what the sellers will take, make one all-cash offer that's low; make one with a little more cash that has terms; and make a third one that's all terms, offering even more money.

Here's what can happen when you put in three offers. In your negotiations, you find out that the sellers want $87,000 for the house—that's their rock-bottom price. First you offer them $87,000 cash. Second, you offer $89,000, putting $2,000 down and paying $700 a month. Then you offer $91,000 with zero down and $799 a month. Work these numbers so they make sense for you and your cash flow. Remember that you're always after a good deal, so start at 20 to 30 percent below market, even on your highest offer. Do you see how your chances for getting one of those offers accepted just went up? Plus, you've differentiated yourself from other potential buyers because you're offering various solutions.

Say the sellers won't negotiate. You're trying lots of ways to build rapport and find out the least amount they'll take, and they won't talk to you. Your backup plan is to shoot them an offer that comes with a time limit: "This offer is only good for 48 hours, two business days from now. It will expire on Friday at noon. I'm looking at 10 other properties." This added pressure helps to limit the possibility that the sellers will shop the contract among other prospective buyers. Try it in the right situation.

Mistake # 32

Spending Too Much Money on a House That You Bought to Fix Up and Sell

To take all the emotion out of real estate, you need to ask three questions when you're deciding whether a property is a good deal:

- What's it going to sell for? (Not what it's appraised for, but what it's going to sell for today.)
- What will repairs cost?
- What can I buy it for?

Remember, we're not speculators. We're investors. We're not betting that a property's value is going to go up next year or in five years. We want a deal that is 20 to 30 percent below what the property is worth today. Those deals are out there.

To answer the first question about the selling price, use comps for three to five comparable sales to learn about market pricing. You can get this information from the Internet (www.Homegain.com, www.Realtor.com). Find all the houses that sold around the property. Make comparisons, apples to apples, of properties sold in the past few months. I can't use a computer, so I pay real estate agents to give me comps, and in return, I give them business. File those comps systematically so that when you go to a bank or wholesale the property to someone else, your file tells them what the property's worth.

Also, call someone such as a real estate agent or investor who's active in the market and verify the comps. For instance, an active investor in a specific neighborhood might confirm that houses do comp out at those prices, but that the market is slow. Or an agent who sells a lot of houses in that area might say that even though they comp out at $300,000, people are only paying $275,000. Or they both might say that it's a hot area, and three buyers will pay $310,000 for the house right now. Get comps and verify the numbers from more than one source.

The second thing to do to determine whether a property is a good deal is to find out how much it will cost to fix it up. Most of the properties you look at, even new homes, need repairs. Who gives you information on repair costs? A contractor. When you go to a banker or want to wholesale a property, lenders will ask what it needs in repairs. They want to know how you came up with the number you're asking for, so work with licensed, bonded, referred contractors and get written bids from them. Pay them for their time and refer business to them. (Referring people can provide another lucrative income stream.)

To get a good deal and arrive at a price you're willing pay, be sure to ask for the seller's lowest price at least three times. Say something like, "I don't like to negotiate, I'm not good at it, I know you don't either—so without negotiating or haggling, what's the absolute least you'd take and be okay?" "Now, let me ask you one other question; I don't like to negotiate. Seriously, what's the least you'd take and be okay?" "I know you're going to make some money, but let me ask this one last question: Can you do any better?" In 45 seconds, a seller might come down from $109,000 to $105,000 to $104,000—that's $5,000 in less than a minute. That would make a pretty good hourly wage! You make your money in real estate through negotiating, especially in tight markets. Disarm the seller by asking the right questions.

When I bought a commercial building and negotiated the price down by $4,000, it took three days. As you negotiate, don't fall into the trap of filling any silence in the conversation with meaningless words. When I'm on the phone negotiating a deal, I'm relaxed and reading a book. I let the other person break the silence. My behavior is based on the principle that the less you care about closing the deal, the more you'll make. Don't get attached to any property; learn the art of negotiation. (See Appendix C.)

Mistake # 33

Analyzing Properties Too Much and Too Long

This is when you spend a year looking at various properties and don't make any offers. Some call it "paralysis of analysis." The message is simple: Get started. Every beginner should have the goal of putting in an offer in the first 30 days and making at least one deal within 90 days. The hardest deal for anyone, including myself, is the first one. Get it out of the way, even if you don't make a lot of money on it.

Say you've made a terrible deal and you lose $1,000. It's still probably the best investment you'll ever make or the least expensive real-life real estate seminar you'll ever attend. I promise you'll do better on your tenth deal than on your first, and better on your fifteenth deal than on your tenth. Focus on the activity that's going to get you your first deal, which is the toughest. Set an activity goal, even if it's shooting out some low offers with a contingency clause (completion of the contract is contingent on the buyer's inspection and approval, on getting favorable financing, etc.) so that you can legally get out of the contract. Make some offers. Get a contract and make more offers. That's the first step. If your offer is accepted, then do your due diligence.

Most of us are scared to make the offers that would get our businesses going. Let's stop doing the business backward right now. That means you're doing your entire due diligence—learning everything about real estate and the property—before you move forward. That adds to your fear and paralysis.

Here's a parallel example. I used to work on Wall Street for a major investment banking firm. The president of our division told me that the firm was going to buy a $300 million company. The analysts had completed their initial research, spent a half a day looking at it, and concluded that it was a good deal if the numbers they had were accurate. As in real estate, you only need to know a few numbers: what the company earns, what its expenses are, and what the industry is like. (It's similar to real estate; the only three numbers you need to know in real estate are what it's worth, what you can get it for, and what the repairs cost. Of course, later you'll want to know about the rents, financing costs, taxes, and insurance. But start by finding out whether the seller is motivated and whether you can get the house for less than what it's worth plus repairs.)

The president of our division wrote a one-page letter stating that his investment firm wanted to buy the target company for $300 million, contingent on inspecting all the books and verifying everything over the next six months. The target company's president read the letter and signed it. Our company sent in accountants and bookkeepers and verified the earnings and expenses, then closed the deal.

That's how it should work in real estate. But if you spend time looking at all the details and verifying them before putting in an offer, you'll likely lose out. In today's competitive market, if you wait, the property will be gone. In some areas of the country, homes sell in a day or even hours.

My approach is to gather those key numbers as quickly as I can, and see if they pass the test. If the seller is motivated, you've negotiated a good price, and you can put it under contract for significantly less than market value, that's a decent deal. Then you put it under contract with a contingency clause, and verify the repair costs with a contractor (who might say that repairs will cost 10 times more than you expected). After that, you decide whether to revise your offer or move on. Making a business decision gets you over your paralysis of analysis.

Remember, you don't need to understand real estate title law or property liens to make an offer. That's the title lawyer's job. You don't need to understand all of the accounting rules. Your accountant will help you with that. You don't need to understand how comps are done to find out what a property is worth. Real estate agents and other investors can help you with that. You don't need to understand everything about asset protection and corporations and land trusts before you make money in real estate. You call your attorney and let him or her set you up with exactly what you need. Do only what you're good at, and let the professionals do what they specialize in.

Mistake # 34

Overlooking Bad Houses and Bad Neighborhoods

Don't be prejudiced against rougher areas. Every town has tough neighborhoods where people get shot, drug dealers sell on the corners, trash litters the yards, cars are jacked up in the front yard, and even police officers are frightened to walk down the street. Remember, you don't have to live there; you don't have to have dinner with your tenants or hang out in the backyard with them. Apply your policies and procedures to determine whether properties in those neighborhoods are good deals, then locate investors in your city who love to buy in those neighborhoods and wholesale houses to them.

Three years ago, a guy wanted to sell me a quadruplex that he had bought for $50,000. Each of the four units would rent for $400 a month, making a total income of $1,600 a month. If he had borrowed $50,000 and could pay it back at a rate of $600 a month with taxes and insurance, that seemed like a good deal: $1,600 coming in, $600 going out. But he wanted to get rid of the property because drug dealers lived there. When I learned that its market value was $85,000, I put it under contract for $45,000—the amount he still owed on his loan. I put a 30-day contingency on the sale when I signed the contract.

I know three people in my town who buy properties in these neighborhoods, so I called them. The first one said, "Robert, that's a bad neighborhood. I buy a lot in war zones, but I'm not going over to *that* one." The second caller said the same thing. The third one, Mikey, owns 400 rental properties in Nashville, packs a pistol, loves collecting rent, and enjoys shootouts. He said this building would have an appraisal value of $90,000, and he'd give me $60,000 for it. I closed the deal with him and made $15,000 for a couple of hours' work.

About two months later, a reporter for a major magazine came to Nashville to interview me. As we were walking on the sidewalk downtown, the couple I bought the quadruplex from happened to be walking toward us. They came up to me and said, "Robert, thank you so much for buying that property from us." The wife hugged me and kissed me. They said, "You have no idea how stressful it was. You've possibly saved our marriage. We thought we were going to die." The reporter thought I'd hired actors just to stage this scene.

This is why I suggest that you *not* overlook bad houses and bad neighborhoods. I'm not telling you what area of real estate is the best for you, because it all can work for you. You can buy and sell single-family homes, apartment buildings, trailers, high end, low end, middle end, commercial property—it all works. Many authors and seminar promoters tell you one specific way to do what they've done (e.g., only do wholesale, only do lease options, only buy and hold, only do rehabs, only do high end, only do three-bedrooms, etc.). Some people make fortunes in all of those categories once they decide to work at it.

But of all the categories in real estate, investors in low-end properties (specifically, trailers) make the highest return on their money. In middle America, I can buy a small house for $50,000 to $80,000 and rent it for $600 to $800. My note or loan is $500; I rent the house for $800; I'm happy making $300 a month. I have buddies who buy 20-year-old trailers for $1,500 to $3,000, then rent them for $100 to $125 a week. They're getting the same amount of rent I'm getting on my $50,000 to $80,000 property, but they have much less money invested. They often sell a trailer on terms, and if the tenant-buyers don't pay, they move the trailer somewhere else. The lower on the economic scale you go, the higher the percentage of the return you'll make. But there's money in high-end properties, too.

Mistake # 35

Not Making Sure Buyers Are Preapproved for a Mortgage

It's a simple but essential step that saves you time and money.

I had 14 duplexes to sell in Nashville, so I ran an ad in the Sunday paper and got 37 responses. The first caller said he wanted to buy all 14 duplexes. I asked if he'd actually seen them. He said, "Absolutely. I know where they are. I know you give good deals. I want to buy them. I'm ready to go. I'll pay cash." My asking price was $1.8 million. I got excited when he called, but I've learned to ask, "Where's the money?" He said it was in the bank. I told him my policy and procedure was not to sign a contract with anyone until they'd been preapproved for financing or had written proof of approval or cash, so I asked him to fax me the bank statement proving he had the cash. He agreed, but he never faxed it, because he simply didn't have it.

The second, third, and fourth callers who responded to my ad weren't serious, but the fifth caller said he was preapproved at a bank. I called his bank and learned that he had applied for a loan, but it wasn't approved yet, maybe in another week or two. I put his application on hold. If I had signed a contract with him during this time, I would have taken the property off the market for 30 to 40 days until his approval came through—*if* it came through. I didn't want to waste time.

The sixth caller said he was preapproved at a bank. When I called his bank to verify this, the representative confirmed it and faxed over a written preapproval letter. We closed on the property 30 days later. The lesson is clear: Never sign a contract until you have written proof that the buyer has been preapproved for financing.

Besides the monetary considerations, be kind to people. You don't want to break their hearts. Typically, after home buyers sign a contract, they tell everyone they know that they just bought a house. Yet half of the time, the deal falls through 30 or 40 days later. That's another reason to ensure that buyers are preapproved before you sign a contract with them.

Mistake # 36

Using Only Short-Term Financing

When I first got into real estate, I was held up by paralysis of analysis. I spent one year and interviewed 200 tenants and 200 real estate investors. Imagine that—before I made one offer, I talked with 400 people! I learned a lot. The number-one mistake investors said they'd made was using only short-term financing. They'd go to the bank, get a one-year loan, and renew it—repeatedly. In 1986, that all changed. The banks shut off the spigot and were calling all the loans in. That could happen again. Now, I don't work with short-term financing if I'm going to hold property (though if I'm getting in and out quickly, that's okay). Don't get all your rentals and rehabs on short-term financing—it's too risky.

Always look at the worst-case scenario. If you were a police officer or soldier, the worst-case scenario would be getting killed. The worst thing that can happen in real estate investing is that you could tie up all your cash in a property, make a bad investment, and lose it all. But if you don't use your own cash, could you lose it? Could you get killed by investing in real estate? Short of being a landlord in a slum neighborhood, probably not. Could you go to jail as a result of being a real estate investor? Not unless you're committing fraud over and over and ripping people off. What's the worst that can happen?

A good friend of mine is one of the biggest real estate investors in the United States. In 1985, he owned more than 20,000 apartment units and had a downtown building that was appraised for $14 million. He owed $10 million on it. Then the real estate market crashed in 1986. The worth of his downtown building sank to $7 million, and he owed more than that on it.

He called his lawyer, who recommended declaring bankruptcy. He didn't like that option, so he drove to the bank with the keys to the building and offered to give it to the bank officers. They didn't want the building, so they renegotiated the loan to $6.5 million. In 2002, he sold that building for $20 million. What a solution! Always ask yourself: What's the worst thing that can happen?

Mistake # 37

Not Having Multiple Sources of Financing so You Can Transact More Deals

I work with some very wealthy investors. One man I know keeps $8 million in his checking account, just in case a deal comes around. That's small change to him, like keeping $100 handy for groceries. He owns thousands of rental units across the country. Whenever I talk with him, the first thing he says is that he can't get enough money. He's got more deals lined up and can't do them because he's always out of money. This can happen when you do real estate!

People tell me that they have a home equity line of credit, backed by a few hundred thousand dollars invested in their home, that they can use to buy more real estate. I tell them not to touch that; it's their home, and *they don't have to touch it.*

If you go to one bank for all your loans, it will stop lending you money. And if you use just one mortgage company, it will stop working with you because you'll hit limits. Sometimes you have to deal with special circumstances, such as when the only bank you deal with doesn't want to make real estate loans anymore. That happened to me; one of the banks that carried loans for 100 of my properties in Nashville had changed names. The bank decided not to carry real estate loans anymore and sold all my loans to someone who wasn't good to work with. I didn't have any control over that. If I didn't have other sources of funds at the time, I'd have been pushed out of business.

In fact, you'll never have enough sources of funding, so you ought to get them now. As a general principle, whenever you need something in business that you don't have, find someone who does. I'm not a good computer repairperson, so I hire someone to do that work for me. I'm not good at accounting, so I hire an experienced accountant.

Similarly, if you don't have good credit, hook up with someone who does. If you don't have oodles of cash, partner with someone who does. If you're self-employed like I am, it can be difficult to borrow money. Even though I have good credit, I have to go to the lender with a wheelbarrow full of tax returns, and it takes a long time to be approved—it's a hassle. So I find someone in my circle who can sashay down to the bank and get loans easily: "Oh, Dr. Smith, just sign here. We'll give you a 100 percent loan at 6 percent for 30 years. Do you need some more? No, we don't need your tax returns because you have a real job with a W-2 and excellent credit."

If you're putting good real estate deals together, it's easy to find people with money through your network. For example, people can lend you money tax-free through their self-directed IRAs. Educate investors about this option. Explain that you can buy houses with their IRAs and sell them; they can lend you money at 8 or 9 percent interest and earn that interest tax-free, secured by real estate.

I like to study supersuccessful investors—people who own more than 200 or 300 properties. One gentleman who owns 1,000 properties has never signed one bank loan and has never borrowed one penny from a mortgage company. His name is not on the title of any of those properties.

You may be thinking, "This won't work, I can't do that. I have to use my own money to buy property." And I reply, "It's worked for him." He gets people to use their self-directed IRAs and pays them 11 percent interest. They own the property; he has a joint agreement. Or they form an LLC, and he owns 50 to 70 percent of it. He makes all the decisions; they get their 11 percent interest, and they're happy about it. Their job is to go to the bank and sign the loans, while his job is to buy, fix, and sell properties. He lets them take most of the depreciation on the properties for their tax returns because he doesn't need it.

Do you know any doctors, lawyers, or businesspeople who wouldn't mind benefiting from the depreciation of those rental properties? In an LLC, you can divide it up.

Most people will put all their own money into their real estate business. They also borrow money from banks. This works, and you can do it this way. But there's a better way.

I challenge you to bring a bank, a mortgage broker, and a hard money-lender into your circle and rely on them. Hard moneylenders are quicker and faster. Sometimes you'll come across deals that can't wait on the bank or the mortgage company or your finance partner, and cash is king. If you can offer cash, you can get better deals.

You may think that you don't want to spend money on hard moneylenders' higher interest rates and points. They charge 10 points on $100,000, which is $10,000—that's a lot of money. But if you're making $30,000 and have to spend $10,000 to get it, you've still made $20,000. Would you sit at a black-jack table if you made $30 every time you put $10 down? You'd probably never leave. You might even ask for a catheter, and say, bring it on, because you're not getting up!

I know so many investors who won't borrow money—declaring that it costs too much—even though they'd make three times whatever they would have spent. I borrow money from hard moneylenders at 10 points and 15 percent interest all the time. I find it's the best money out there.

To buy property you want to hold without using your own money, do this: Get a source of short-term financing (such as a line of credit) to pay cash to buy properties and fix them, then refinance them within a year. Then put them on your program and rent them out or lease-option them.

Mistake # 38

Spending Too Much Time Talking to Tenants, Worrying about Repairs, Doing Paperwork, and Making Very Little Money

I know this mistake well, because I practiced it for four solid years. I managed my own property and was very good at it. No one will ever take care of your business or manage your property as well as you will yourself. However, you need to consider how your time is best spent. I challenge every landlord to think about hiring a property management firm, because even if you're great at it, you are losing money. The time you spend managing could be spent finding and closing deals. Property management isn't fun; it's stressful, time consuming, and unprofitable.

Look at this example. You have a rental that brings in $1,000 a month, and you're managing it yourself. A management firm generally charges 7 to 10 percent of the rent to manage a property. Therefore, at 10 percent, it costs $100 a month to hire a good manager. Now do the math. In the past year, how many trips have you made to the property, how many phone calls have you taken for it, how much time did you spend doing paperwork, orchestrating repairs, and dealing with tenants? You probably spend about five hours a month managing that property, which means you have a $20-an-hour job. Is that why you got into real estate? And how much did the detail work bother you? Managing properties can be stressful. Tenants never call to say thank you for providing this great place they live in. They never send you the rent early. In everyday life, every time a tenant calls, it's because of a problem. I recommend that you hire a management company and manage the manager. That manager may even cost an extra 5 to 10 percent, because he or she won't do it as well as you. But what's your true cost? If it frees your time and you use it to find more deals, it's worth it.

Another good reason to get out of the management business is liability. If you're managing the property, you have direct contact with your tenants; therefore, you're the first person they will sue. And tenants *will* sue. I contend that if you don't have problem tenants or an occasional lawsuit, you don't have enough tenants. The most sued professional category in the world is landlord/property manager, so that's a good business for you to get out of.

Mistake # 39

Not Having a Systematic Way to Run Your Rental Business

When you own rental property, it's critical to set up a system that makes it possible to run your business on autopilot. It will save you enormous amounts of time.

The following areas of my rental business program have worked well over the years:

- Make it a policy to ask questions before meeting with prospective renters. This tells you how responsible they would be as tenants. Often, people don't even show up for their appointments.
- Instead of always being personally available to your tenants or prospective tenants, set up a voice-mail system. Remember, calls from tenants can be frustrating. They never call to say that they want to pay the rent early and they love the property. They call when they want you to deal with a problem.
- When callers phone about your ad in the paper, they get basic information from your voice mail. I've hired a woman with a pleasant British accent to make our voice-mail recordings. The message goes like this: "Thank you for calling Denton Properties. We have a lovely two-bedroom, one-bath home on the rental program. We also have a homeownership program . . ." She tells them everything they want to know about the house on the voice mail. "Press 1 for East Nashville, 2 for South Beach, 3 for Liberty City. . . . Here's how our rental program works. Drive by the property (please do not disturb any people living there), then call the other number to arrange a showing on our rental program. We'd love to work

with you. Thank you. Here's the other number. Be sure to see the property first." Almost everyone calls the other number and gives us the opportunity to explain how our program works.

■ When a prospective tenant calls back, we say, "We'd love to work with you. We want to ask you a few questions. We don't expect you to have a perfect record, but we care about honesty in your answers." (You can find the full script for this interview in my course material, but here are some starting questions.) "First, why are you moving?" We ask this question three times. I study psychology, hypnosis, and Chinese torture techniques; they come in handy in landlording. Psychological studies show that if you ask a question three times, you're more likely to get the truth. So we have imbedded in our script three times, "Why are you moving?" Here's one answer we've received: "I've lived in the same property for 12 years, my landlord sold it, and I need to move." Great. We give 100 out of 100 points for that answer. Another answer is, "We really need a place today." Watch out. Most likely, these people have just been evicted.

■ We always ask, "How long have you lived in the place you live now? How long did you live in the place before that?" Their answers give you a good prediction of how long they'll live in your place, too.

■ We inform prospective tenants that we do a credit and criminal background check on everyone who will live in our properties, and we ask them, "What will we find?" About 10 percent of the time, they stop talking and hang up. Other landlords who don't ask that question might meet them at a property and rent to them, but don't waste your time. In fact, doing this can even be dangerous. One landlord friend of mine met a prospective renter at a vacant house. That prospect shot my friend in the head. Thankfully, the bullet went out through his cheek, and he's okay today.

■ Be sure to carefully screen people over the phone and meet them in groups at your convenience. Then, once they've signed the application, do thorough background checks. That's how you'll find out if they're lying to you.

- Meet potential renters at your convenience. And since people are often late, tell them you'll meet them at 5:00 P.M., but you'll leave at 5:10 if they're not there. Chances are they'll show up by 5:15. That's not perfect, but it's better than waiting 45 minutes or more. Carry something to read or make good use of your time in other ways, because you're likely to be kept waiting.
- Rent is due on the first of the month and late on the fifth; we evict on the eleventh. People call me all the time to tell me they lost their jobs and want a break. Our policy and procedure allows them to send us a written plan for how they will pay the rent. By the way, the eviction process takes 30 days. We don't tell them this, knowing that we can always stop the process at any time.

For any business, having policies and procedures is a benefit because they remove the need for daily decision making. I suggest that you put everything you do in real estate into a program. Take your emotions out of the middle, and run your program systematically. You won't get frustrated or stressed out if you have in place the three Ps: *policies, procedures,* and *program.*

Mistake # 40

Not Setting Up Minimum Standards in Writing When Selecting Tenants

If you don't set up written minimum standards as a landlord, you could be found guilty of violating fair-housing regulations. The law requires that you rent or lease-option to the first person who meets your written minimum standards. The government routinely sends out officials to test for discrimination, and you could be tagged, especially if you own a large number of rentals, as I do.

The fines for violating fair-housing regulations start at $15,000 per incident, which is a good reason to set up minimum standards. But what often happens in the process of selecting tenants? Studies show that 58 percent of small property owners base their decisions about accepting new tenants on looks, likeability, and first impressions. They think, "He's a nice guy, looks serious and sincere, and has cash in hand." Your prospective renter may even have something in common with you. But if you take action based on biased criteria, you're guilty of discrimination. Numbering your applications, for example, helps you prove that you've selected those who first meet your standards.

I actually include politeness as a minimum standard. What characteristics you include is up to you, but be sure to take into account the laws in your state. Race, creed, national origin, color, disability, and family status are protected classes.

Mistake # 41

Not Charging Tenants for Damages to Your Property

In my opinion, the only damages owners should be responsible for are normal wear and tear; tenants should pay for any damages they create.

About 90 percent of the time when I send my plumber to fix a broken toilet, he pulls out Beanie Babies, hairbrushes, and more. Who should be paying for that? The tenant. So when tenants move into my properties, they sign a damage disclaimer in addition to the lease. This disclaimer says, "You and your guests are responsible for the damages you cause: This is an estimate of costs, it may cost more." Then, if a leaky sink costs $75 to fix, I charge tenants $150. If a doorjamb costs $80, I charge them $160. (I like to keep things simple and multiply by two.) Most repairs include holes in the wall, stains in the carpet, leaky sinks, broken toilets, missing window screens, and so on. Start charging your tenants for damages, and you will save money. I can't always collect on everything, but unpaid damages become unpaid security deposits.

Mistake # 42

Not Screening Tenants Well Enough

Always do a credit and criminal background check. Ask how long they've lived in the place they're living in now *and* the one before that. Check with at least two previous landlords.

Because it's become easier to qualify for a home loan in the past few years, the pool of people who rent has become smaller and less desirable. Screening becomes more important than ever. My office actually checks with three previous landlords to make sure we know the tenants' history.

Say that George, a prospective tenant, deals drugs, fires machine guns, and never pays the rent on time. He's currently renting from Ron. Now Ron is an honest guy, but when I call him for a reference about George, Ron is eager to get rid of his nightmare tenant and says, "He's great! I'll help him move this weekend!" Then I find out by calling Sue, George's landlord before Ron, that George tore the place up and never paid the rent. Since George doesn't live in her property anymore, Sue is more likely to be straightforward and say, "He's a nightmare; don't rent to him." That's why it's important to check with at least two landlords, preferably three.

Mistake # 43

Not Doing a Credit and Criminal Background Check on Everyone Who Receives a Key to Your Property

Before you rent to a tenant, do a background check, or you'll definitely regret it. If you're using the same contractors or repair people repeatedly and want to give them a key, run a background check on them, too.

Say a person you hired robs, rapes, pillages, and plunders your tenants, and consequently gets arrested. When the police find out you hired him and didn't do a background check—and their background check tells them he just got out of jail for raping someone—they'll hold you responsible.

I've been ripped off by a contractor who had finished two jobs well, then took my money and ran on the third. Clearly, he had a confidence scam going. Later, I found out that he'd done the same thing 60 other times in 12 states. If I'd done a criminal check on him, I'd have discovered that he had 18 judgments against him from every real estate company in the southeastern United States.

You want to know that people you're giving a $10,000 contract to are financially stable, so do a credit check on them, too. Let them pay the $20 it costs to have a service check their credit. Check people out before you hire them, before you give them money, and especially before you give them a key to your property. Make this a strict policy and procedure.

Mistake # 44

Not Having a High Enough Cash Flow from Your Rental Properties

The number-one complaint of landlords is not making enough money because repairs cut into their cash flow. Rental properties usually have a 30 to 40 percent vacancy and repair rate; also, every time a tenant moves, you have to paint, fix the carpet, and absorb costs if the unit sits empty for a month or two. You'll never make as much money from your rental property as you'd like because of vacancies and repairs.

To deal with low cash flow because of high repair costs, get out of the repair business. My rental company used to provide all our rental units with a refrigerator, stove, and sometimes a window air conditioner. Every day, we'd get calls to repair these: $50 here, $80 there. So we got out of the appliance business. If the appliance is already in the property, we'll lend it to the tenants. If it breaks and they won't fix it, we'll come and pick it up. We make it clear in the lease that the appliances don't come with the rental, and that has saved us a lot of money.

At one point, I decided we should get out of the repair business entirely. We did that by first setting a repair minimum. Most of the repairs cost $50 to $100 for leaky sinks and broken toilets. Our policy says that the tenants pay for the first $100 to $300 in repairs. When they sign the lease, they also sign a paper that says they're responsible for basic repairs. This works like an insurance deductible and is based on no-fault maintenance laws. (Be sure to find out if no-fault maintenance is legal is your state.)

Another way to get out of the repair business entirely is through lease optioning. When they rent to own, tenant-buyers have pride of ownership.

State in your lease-option agreement that they're responsible for repairs, at least up to a certain amount. I recommend making them responsible for up to $1,000, because your insurance should already cover big repairs such as fixing the roof. When you screen prospective tenant-buyers, make sure they're capable of doing the repairs, then verify that they're actually getting them done. If they ignore a leaky sink, for example, a $50 repair becomes a $5,000 kitchen rehab because you're dealing with rotted floorboards.

Generally, renters don't take good care of things. If you've ever rented a car, you've probably taken the turns fast, thrown soda cans in the backseat, and run over the curbs. Would you ever do that in your own car? Not likely. Don't be shocked that your tenants tear up the property—they're renting it. That's another reason to make them owners through lease-option, rent-to-own home buying: They take care of the home as owners would. They may call and ask if they can plant flowers, put a deck in the back, install a pool, and so on. In your lease, make it a requirement that they have to call and get an approval for any improvements or repairs. If you agree to an upgrade, make sure they hire a good contractor to build anything that would stay in the event that they leave. You don't want to be saddled with big problems that they've created. Most of the time, I love it when our tenant-buyers make improvements.

Mistake # 45

Penalizing Bad Tenants but Not Rewarding Good Ones

When you're renting, you evict the bad tenants who don't pay and charge them for any damages, as you should. But what do you do to reward good tenants? Every time a tenant moves, it costs you $1,000 to $15,000 because of vacancies, repairs, and overhead—plus the stress of dealing with them moving out. It makes sense to find ways to keep your renters by setting up a retention program. Advertise this program to attract good tenants in the first place, and get your tenants excited about it.

How long do you want your tenants to stay? I want our good tenants to stay at least 30 years, until the mortgages are paid off. So we have programs in writing that we show new tenants up front. If they stay with us two or three years, pay the rent on time, and don't do any damage, we give them an incentive—a refrigerator, a trip, a cruise, a $100 or $200 bonus. We might do an improvement on the property—a carpet cleaning, a new ceiling fan. Tenants get to pick from a list we provide.

I call a lot of my tenants nomads, because, like the nomads in the desert, they move around all the time. When their leases are up, they tend to move for no reason. When tenants tell us they're moving, we ask them why. About 50 percent of the time, the reasons are absolutely ridiculous: They don't like the neighbor's dog or kids; the brother who lives eight doors down bothers them. We tell them we'll try to do something about it and send a letter to the people they're complaining about. After we do this, our tenants often stay. At times, they're unhappy with something about the house—say, the carpet in the back bedroom is dirty—so we keep them as tenants by paying $30 to clean a carpet.

Most landlords and property management companies tell a tenant who's moving, "Great, leave the key. You might get your deposit back. See you later." But it pays for us to take the time to interview our tenants and ask, "Why are you moving? Why are you moving? Why are you moving?" We want them to stay, and we make it easy if we can.

I learned from Mr. Landlord (www.Mrlandlord.com) that the most serious complaint tenants have against their landlords is that the landlord doesn't make repairs. We now offer a three- to five-day repair guarantee. When tenants move in, we show them this written guarantee that's in the form of a certificate. The guarantee says that if the tenant calls about a repair and we're responsible for it, we'll fix it in three to five business days. If we fail to fix it within that time, we'll give them their daily rent back in cash for every day it's not fixed. That's a radical promise, but it gives us an edge in the rental market. New tenants choose our properties over other rentals because of it.

In reality, tenants rarely remember our guarantee, so they're surprised when they receive a check and letter in the mail. The letter says, "Mr. Smith, you called in on Monday; our repair person messed up and didn't get there until Friday. We apologize. We have a three-day repair guarantee. Here's $60, your two days of rent in cash. We're sorry and we hope it doesn't happen again. Have a great time on our money. Thanks." We regularly have a waiting list of 100 tenants, even in a soft rental market, because we treat tenants like valued customers.

If tenants declare they're going to move, we send them a letter that outlines all the expenses they will incur in moving: utility deposits, new rental deposit, moving truck, loss of work. We add up the costs—over $2,000—and send them the letter. Seeing the total cost serves to make them think twice about moving.

If you hate being a landlord because the tenants always bug you with their problems, get out of the rental management business. The first step is to hire a qualified property management company; the second step is to learn about lease optioning and start turning your tenants into home buyers.

SUCCESSFUL REAL ESTATE INVESTING

Mistake # 46

Not Learning about Government Programs for Low-Income Tenants

If you're in the low- and moderate-income rental market, learn about the Section 8 program for low-, moderate-, and fixed-income people. Through this program, the federal government pays part of the rent. Participation in this program requires that your properties be inspected. The inspections are tough, but once your properties pass them and you do the paperwork, the government pays all or most of the rent, guaranteed. And you still have the right to screen the tenants who move into your properties.

A Section 8 program lets you apply the Section 8 payments from the government toward your mortgage payment. It's designed to convert Section 8 renters into home buyers and allows you to lease-option your properties to them. Go to your local Section 8 office and talk to other Section 8 landlords about this. Always get referrals to see how the program works and learn about the advantages and disadvantages.

I also rent properties to nonprofit organizations. They want living spaces for clients who have special needs: people with physical and mental disabilities, chronic incapacitating diseases, and so on. These nonprofit organizations not only pay the rent but also help to maintain the properties they rent. When their clients move out, they are responsible for repairing any damage. That's stated in the lease. Do you see the advantages that come with renting to nonprofits? You get good tenants and free property management. You also get out of the rent-collection business.

Mistake # 47

Not Inspecting Properties Regularly

This applies to lease optioners, landlords, rehabbers, and silent owners. It may shock you to hear this, but there is no such thing as a bad tenant. If there were no bad landlords, there would be no bad tenants.

A few years ago I had a tenant who did $18,000 in damages to my duplex, which was what it was worth. Whose fault was that? Mine. If I'd followed my own policies and procedures, I wouldn't have incurred that damage.

I didn't screen the tenant properly, and I didn't get a landlord reference. If I'd done these two things, I wouldn't have rented to her, because I learned too late that she'd destroyed the unit she lived in before. In the first month, she did $800 worth of damage to my duplex, destroying the carpet and dirtying the place. In the second month, she did another $2,000 or $3,000 worth of damage. But I didn't inspect it until the eighth month. By then, there was $18,000 worth of damage. If I had inspected in the first 30 days, I would have stopped the damage at $800.

I recommend inspecting every single one of your properties every 30 days, whether you own it, lease it, lease-option it, or rely on a management company to manage it. If you don't, you will be surprised. If you had a $100,000 jewelry piece, wouldn't you pull it out every now and then to look at it? If you had a $100,000 sports car in your garage, wouldn't you go look at it every few weeks, even if you weren't going to drive it? You've got a $100,000 property—please look at it. When you inspect your property every 30 days, the tenants will know you're serious about caring for it, the managers will know you're checking up on them, and it will help you take care of your investment.

About every five weeks, I fly to Nashville and inspect every one of my units myself. It takes me a day to look at hundreds of units. My leases say that someone from my rental company can go in on the second Tuesday of the month, during normal business hours. We're going to come in and inspect for repairs and maintenance. We may check the air conditioner, change the air filter, spray for bugs. The tenants are given notice that we're coming in. Remember, you cannot go in without giving your tenants some type of notice; it's their residence.

Mistake # 48

Attempting to Perform Your Own Evictions and Collections, and Getting Sued

I'm an attorney; I could do my own evictions. But I don't. And I don't recommend that you do, either.

Say your tenants move out. They've left the property, and they owe you money. You enter the property and see that they've left one tennis shoe and an old toothbrush behind, and you throw out these items. With that action, you've just broken the law. This happened to a friend of mine. He was sued and lost $40,000 because the tenants said they'd never moved out, and the judge backed their argument. Remember, until your tenants have relinquished 100 percent control, the residence is their home by law. You can't enter it unless you've given them written notice.

Because landlords tend to have money and tenants don't, landlords are usually found guilty in disputes that go to court. Make sure you follow the law, and hire a good, qualified eviction and collection attorney. Every time a situation comes up, call your attorney before you do anything. Be sure to document every contact you have with your tenants.

Maybe you're pursuing a judgment to evict the tenants and get your house back, but you're not succeeding in collecting the thousands of dollars they owe you. You're also not marking their credit, so when they rent another place, their credit report doesn't show the eviction. A good eviction and collection attorney will hound them for the next 7 to 10 years. The attorney will do a skip trace, and if those tenants ever get other jobs, the attorney will garnish their income. It may take months or years, but you'll eventually get your money, in most cases. Your local apartment association or real estate investors association can refer you to some good collection attorneys. Many good collection attorneys charge one-third of the amount that they collect.

When you communicate with your tenants, tell them, "You're going to pay this money. It doesn't matter to me how you pay it. I'm just the lowly, underpaid manager. Today you owe $1,000, but tomorrow, it's going to go to the eviction attorneys. When it goes to them, they're going to tack on fees and fines and court costs, and it will grow to $1,800 or more. The lawyers will come after you for seven years. If you get a job, they'll garnish your income. If you ever own a house, they'll put a lien on it. If you ever get any money, they'll come after that, too. Take your pick—pay your rent or get evicted." (In eviction, the court declares that the tenants have to leave. If they don't, the sheriff comes out to remove them. The sheriff is the *only* person who can remove someone from a rental property.)

Once a dispute goes to the eviction attorneys, landlords are not allowed to talk to the tenants, so remove yourself from the process completely. Evictions can be nasty and you don't want to get involved in them.

My rental company's policy is that our rent is due on the first, late on the fifth, and we evict on the eleventh. Most landlords wait three months to file for eviction. If you wait, though, you're going to regret it. If your tenants can't pay one month's rent, they won't be able to pay two months' rent—it's business.

Mistake # 49

Not Using Licensed, Bonded, and Referred Contractors and Repair People

If you're going to hire contractors and repair people, and if you want to avoid lawsuits, treat them as you would a doctor: Make sure you have references, make sure you've checked them out, and make sure you (and they) know what they're doing. If they do poor work and aren't licensed and bonded, you'll be held responsible. Make sure they carry proper insurance. To verify their coverage, get documentation from them showing that they're currently insured and licensed, or call the appropriate state department or association to find out.

When I started out in real estate, I hired a contractor who said he was licensed, bonded, and insured—and it said so on his truck, too. Two years later, when his employees sued him after being injured on the job, they found out he wasn't licensed, bonded, or insured at all. They started coming after me as the property owner. Please don't get caught up in a mess like that.

Mistake # 50

Paying Too Much for Repairs and Not Getting Written Bids

Insist on written bids for repair work that include a completion date and a total dollar cost, or repair costs could ruin your real estate business. I'm not talking about just losing $100 here and there. If you rehab residential properties (on which you might spend $30,000 for repairs) or even a commercial property (on which you might spend $600,000 for repairs), you could lose thousands to tens of thousands of dollars. To avoid being ripped off or taken advantage of, use only referred repair people or contractors. If they're not referred but can give you references, be sure to make the phone calls and check out the quality of their work and the competitiveness of their pricing. If they don't have two or three good verifiable references, don't deal with them. Check with your local real estate association for referrals and warnings about which contractors to stay away from.

For your own protection, get every repair bid in writing. Every detail—every doorstop, every paint job, even the cleanup—should be listed, with a specific completion date. Have the contractor break costs down into materials and labor, then take time to verify the material costs with a few phone calls to suppliers so you know they're reasonable. To check labor time, divide the estimated time by the total amount and calculate an hourly rate.

Call other contractors and investors to check what hourly rate is reasonable in your market.

Generally, you get what you pay for. Every time I've negotiated someone down to accept a lower hourly rate, I've regretted it. If the price is too low, contractors don't have enough money in the job to cover overhead costs and still make a profit.

Mistake # 51

Paying for a Repair or Construction Job before It's 100 Percent Completed

I used to get ripped off by contractors. After five years of losing hundreds of thousands of dollars, I decided to research successful people and imitate what they do. When governments prepare contracts for multimillion-dollar construction projects, they include a provision that I suggest you include in all of yours: a 10 to 20 percent holdback. This means that payment of 10 to 20 percent of the entire amount is held back until the repair job is 100 percent completed—*including* the cleanup.

I had hired a contractor to do a $60,000 rehab on a house I'd purchased. After working on it for six weeks, the contractor said he had just finished and wanted his payment. I called my inspector, who told me the work looked good, but two doors were off their hinges and trash had been left in the yard. I couldn't sell or rent it like that, so I called the contractor at 4 P.M. on a Friday. He knew I was holding back $12,000—that is, 20 percent of the total he was owed. Guess when he went to put on the two doors and clean the yard? At 4:12 P.M. that same day. If I had paid him all the money, he wouldn't have come back.

Mistake # 52

Not Having a per-Day Penalty for Contract Work That's Not Finished When Promised

Make sure you set up a per-day penalty for work that's completed after the deadline. This makes a big difference in getting what you want in a timely manner.

Here's a good example. I bought a five-bedroom, three-bath property in the historic district for $18,000. It needed $18,000 in repairs. I put a total of $36,000 into this house, and it was appraised for $95,000. I saw that as a good deal—a home run. My contractor friend said he'd have the repair work done in six to eight weeks—drywall, paint, carpet, air-conditioning, and kitchen work. Since he was my friend, I gave him almost all of the payment up front. Unfortunately, it took him a year to complete the job, because he spent time on other jobs, too. So, instead of having $36,000 invested in it, I had the cost of capital, carrying costs, stress, headache, time, phone calls, overhead, insurance, taxes, liability—more than $50,000 worth of hassles. When he was finally finished, I called my Realtor (I love working with real estate agents!) and said, "I want to blow this property out the door. Even though it's worth $95,000 with all the work done, let's blow it out at $75,000." I just wanted to make $25,000 and move on; I was tired of dealing with it.

My agent held an open house the first weekend, and 33 people showed up. They all loved the house, but no one made an offer. Why? To them, the price seemed too cheap, so they thought something must have been wrong with the house. Then we raised the price to $94,900 and sold it in three weeks, possibly to the same people who saw it when it was priced at $75,000. The lesson, in addition to not prepaying the contractor, is to never show or rent a home until it's 100 percent finished, and to price it right.

Mistake # 53

Assuming That the Way You Think and Do Business Is the Way Other People Think and Do Business

I hope that you are an honest person, one who lives up to your commitments. You do what you say you're going to do and know that other people can trust you. More than likely, if this is how you are, you think that most everyone else is like you. Be careful! Watch out! Never assume that anyone you do business with thinks or acts as you do or in ways you want them to.

Although you will meet incredible, helpful, honest people throughout your real estate investing career, there are also a lot of crooks. Contractors, tenants, lenders, property managers, real estate agents, and other investors sometimes won't do what they promise. Stuff happens, and you may come across some completely dishonest people. Therefore, always protect yourself with the proper paperwork and financial controls. In addition:

- Trust your instincts.
- Verify everything people tell you by calling a third party.
- Get references on anyone and everyone you will be working with.
- Make sure your policies and procedures protect you, and do not violate them.
- Get *everything* in writing: every promise or commitment to fix, sell, manage, partner, close, share, or help. Get it *in writing*.

Mistake # 54

Selling Your Property Instead of Holding It

This may or may not be a mistake, but many older, seasoned investors tell me that their biggest mistake was selling their properties.

Please understand that holding property is work, takes upkeep, and sometimes can cost you. However, if you are able, you may want to hold your property longer than you think. Of course, if an area where you own property is deteriorating, you may want to get out. What will the property be worth 5, 10, or 20 years from now? What about a house that you owned a share of 20 or 30 years ago? What is it worth today? Remember that you only make a lot of money in real estate when you *sell* or *refinance*. Your monthly income may be okay or good or excellent, but the real money is made when you sell or refinance. Perhaps, instead of selling, you might want to refinance and pull some of your equity out. To raise some cash, you could also sell a part of your property to a money partner instead of selling all of it. You need to at least think about your goals and what you are giving up by selling a property. What could or would its future appreciation really be? What is the time value of the future profit?

Also, if you sell, you may have to pay taxes on the gains, if you do not do a 1031 Tax-Free Exchange. Often when you refinance a property, you don't pay taxes on the money that you pull out. Please consult a good tax accountant who works with real estate investors for an analysis of the tax consequences of selling versus refinancing. The key question is: Should your property stay or go? If you keep it, it could be trouble; if you sell, it could be double.

One of the houses I bought and kept for two years was a great deal. I bought it for about $150,000 and spent $50,000 to repair it. I had about

$200,000 in it and sold it for $303,000—a $100,000 profit in two years. When I sold it, it was one of the most expensive houses in the area. That is, my real estate friends thought its price was at the top of the market. Four years later, that same house listed for about $680,000. What to do? What to do? Of course, never worry too much about whether to keep a property or sell it if you're making money on it.

Mistake # 55

Relying on What People Tell You, Not on What They *Do*

Are you ready for a secret that will help you avoid a lot of mistakes and save you a ton of money and headaches? My father often says, "The only problem with business is that there are people involved." Every business, especially real estate, is a "people" business. The more you can understand, relate to, and learn about people in real estate, the better. Here's one of the secrets that I have learned: *Map your reality on what people* do, *not what they* say.

I used to, and still do, sometimes rely on and believe everything people tell me. I know that you do this, too. "The house will be painted in 10 days." "The loan will be approved and closed by the end of the month." "All of the rest will be paid this Friday." "Don't worry, it is taken care of." It's not that people who tell you one thing and do another are bad. More often than not, they mean well and just want you to feel good. However, all of our frustrations in life and business come from only one occurrence: *Our expectations are not met.*

For example, the tenants told you the rent would be paid on time; you expected them to pay it, they wanted to pay you, but they did not. You are now frustrated. So, reduce your frustration level. Don't rely on what people say; only rely on and map on what they do. This will lower your expectations, and your frustration level will go way down, too. Start applying this in all areas of your life and especially real estate.

Think back to a frustrating situation in your life. Think about how you would have felt if you'd only mapped your reality by the other people's

111

actions, not their *words.* Your expectations then (and moving forward) should be zero until they prove themselves—not by telling but by doing. Would you have felt differently? How? What would you have done differently?

I believe there are two types of people in life, *talkers* and *doers.* Which one are you? This is a great question to ask yourself and everyone you work with. Of course, you don't have to ask them out loud.

Mistake # 56

Letting Fear and Hesitation Keep You from Getting the Deal

Every real estate beginner and pro has lost and will lose deals by not moving fast enough. To avoid that result, you need to focus on the following actions:

- Finding a motivated seller.
- Doing your initial quick three-part analysis:

  What is the property worth today?
  What will the repairs cost?
  What is a good purchase price with a realistic margin for profit?

Then focus on getting a *signed contract* immediately. Until you have a signed contract, you have nothing. After you have a signed contract, your next focus should be on *closing* on the property. You should close whether you are going to hold it, fix it and sell it, or wholesale it. Look at your possible deals every day to focus yourself. Make sure that your activities are intended to achieve these goals. Keep a checklist on a large board and track your activity. Check off each step of the process as you achieve it. After you have some experience, you can go through this process quickly.

One day, a penthouse unit came on the market in my building in South Beach, Florida. I contacted the sellers that day and found out that they were highly motivated because they'd moved and couldn't afford payments on both their new home and this one. A real estate friend ran the comparable sales for me. She verified that the unit was worth about $800,000, with no repairs to be made. That afternoon, I put in an offer for $677,000, which they said they'd probably accept. I also offered to lease with an option to buy for $3,400 a month and an option price of $699,000, with 30 percent of the rent going toward the purchase. This entire process took about three hours of phone calls, verifications, and offer writing. By the way, I can be lazy, so I had my real estate friend draw up all of the paperwork. The sellers had only 48 hours to respond.

Every hour and every day, ask yourself these questions: What is my focus? Is this the best use of my time? If I could get this property for $699,000, it certainly was a good way to spend my time.

Mistake # 57

Not Choosing and Working with Partners Wisely

So many real estate investors get together with a friend or relative and decide to start buying property. They have the best intentions, but unfortunately, they soon begin to argue, their business suffers, and their relationship might be forever damaged. Be careful about whomever you get into business with. Make sure they have verifiable skills that will help you. Check their references, even if you think you know them. Remember, this a business, so treat it as such.

As you determine who you want to partner with, write out each person's business duties, job description, and time lines for getting things done. Recognize that it's rare to have an equal partnership, even in a marriage; usually one spouse makes most of the decisions in certain areas. You and your real estate partners must be able to make good, quick decisions. Therefore, decide who takes charge of which areas and determine upfront when and how you will communicate with each other. I always recommend communicating in writing—e-mails or faxes—so you automatically create a record you can refer back to if there's any confusion about who said what.

Here's a checklist for selecting and working with partners:

- Check references and skill levels.
- Detail in writing each person's job description and area of authority.
- Put all agreements in writing.
- Hire an attorney to draw up or approve your agreements.

- Decide how best to borrow money and take title to the property or properties to protect everyone's interests.
- Make sure that all parties are named in the insurance policies on the property or properties.
- Have an exit strategy to get out of the business if things change or someone wants out. Businesses are often easier to get into than out of.

Mistake # 58

Not Understanding How to Deal
with Real Estate Agents as an Investor

Real estate agents can be an investor's best friend. They should be an important part of your business, helping you with almost every aspect of it. They find good deals, write contracts, sell properties, and facilitate almost every aspect of the deals you make. When you buy a listed property, the seller of that property usually pays the agent's commission, so it may not even cost you directly to have an agent on your team. If you sell a property, then you, as the seller, pay the agent's commission, which generally ranges from 6 to 7 percent of the property's selling price.

I highly recommend that you find a few good real estate agents to become part of your team. As with retaining any professional, interview them, get references, and understand who they represent. Some agents represent sellers; some represent buyers; some can represent both.

Remember that real estate investing is a different business from being an agent or broker. Agents earn commissions by helping list properties for sale and by helping buyers purchase properties. In contrast, investors look for good deals on properties, buy them, wholesale them, lease option them, fix them up, and sell them—using all types of creative acquisition, financing, and sales techniques. If an agent doesn't regularly work with investors, you may hear that person say such things as, "You can't do this here." If your child or loved one needed an operation, you would find a seasoned professional doctor with excellent references and the right specialization credentials. Do the same with real estate agents and anyone else you work with. Go to investment associations, talk with other investors, call real estate companies, and find, interview, and screen those recommended. You're searching for agents who understand you and what you're looking for.

At times, some professionals—doctors, lawyers, accountants, contractors, and agents—forget that they're working for you. You're the one in control as the client.

I recommend that you get a written plan from your real estate agents regarding how they would systematically find deals for you. For example, they might say that once a week, they'll scan the multiple-listing service for expiring listings, signs of motivated sellers, out-of-state owners, low mortgage balances on high-equity properties, and so on. Get a written plan for how they would market and sell your properties, too, using advertising, open houses, brochures and fliers, signage, and so on. Expect professionalism from them.

Mistake # 59

Not Understanding the Difference between Being a Real Estate *Investor* and a Real Estate *Speculator*

Beware of the distinction between investing and speculating. Real estate *investors* buy properties from motivated sellers at a real discount—that is, the property must be worth at least 20 percent more than the purchase price. Real estate *speculators* buy property for close to full price. For example, if you were a speculator, you'd pay $100,000 for a house worth $103,000 and hope it would go up in value to $120,000 soon. You'd make all of your money when you sold it. This is much riskier than investing, because your profit depends solely on that property increasing in value. You'll make more in the long run by becoming a wise and patient investor.

Many investors, including me, have learned to consistently find deals on properties at 30 to 60 percent below their current market value. Once you've found that deal, you can wholesale it, lease-option it, fix it up and sell it, or rent it out. However, if you buy property for 90 percent or more of its value and the market goes down 5 to 10 percent, you may not be able to sell it profitably. By buying at least 20 percent below market value, you have a built-in cushion in case the market goes down.

Mistake # 60

Not Having Enough Rent Coming in to Cover All of Your *Real* Expenses

Many investors buy property that doesn't have good cash flow. That is, they purchase a home for $200,000, borrow almost all of the money so their payment is $1,800 a month, and rent it out for $2,000 a month. These numbers don't take into account an average vacancy rate of 5 to 10 percent ($100 to $200 a month), expenses, repairs, capital improvements, roof replacement, plumbing repairs, and so on, which can total 20 to 30 percent ($400 to $600 a month).

In addition to the mortgage and any homeowners' fees, you need to calculate office and auto expenses, phone calls, professional services (attorneys, accountants, etc.) as well as your own time. Then you'll figure in taxes, insurance, and possibly other fees. Contact your local apartment association to find out what your local vacancy and repair rates are. Make sure you have a way to track all your expenses accurately.

Your best bet is to calculate and understand all of your expenses up front. Double-verify them *before* you buy a property. Most landlords don't find out that their properties don't have adequate cash flow until *after* they own them.

You might be thinking, "Wait a minute. I have some great tenants who always pay the rent on time, and I've had very few repair expenses." Great. But you're forgetting that roofs, carpets, floors, plumbing, and appliances only last so long. You're wise to start saving and allocating money for these big expenses immediately.

Also remember that when that a good tenant moves out, it will likely take 30 days or more until a new tenant moves in. You will have to clean, paint, and repair the place. If your rent were $1,000 a month, you'd lose a month's rent of $1,000 and have to spend $1,000 to get the unit ready for a new tenant, for a total expense of $2,000.

Your positive cash flow for the whole year can disappear quickly with just one or two big repairs. Make sure you prepare yourself for this eventuality by putting some money in escrow each month. This way, you can afford that repair when the time comes. Don't spend the funds you're certain to need at some time.

Mistake # 61

Not Setting Up Separate Bank Accounts and Accounting for Each of Your Real Estate Activities

Many real estate investors start out by buying, fixing, then perhaps wholesaling properties. Often, the profits from one activity will compensate for losses on another. But you won't see the big picture if you commingle monies.

As you know, one of the most common reasons that businesses—including real estate—fail is because there isn't enough cash in the company. To avoid cash-flow problems, be sure you know what the cash flow is from each of your activities. Have a separate bank account and accounting system for each aspect of your real estate business.

For many years, I made the mistake of commingling my rental property expenses and income with my rehabbing (that is, fixing and selling houses, not drug or alcohol rehab) income and expenses. Some of my rental properties didn't have very good cash flow. However, when I sold a house and made several thousand dollars, this influx would replenish the account and mask the problems with some of my rentals. If I'd separated each activity into separate accounts, the financial picture would have been much clearer.

The time to set up a separate and proper accounting system for your real estate business is now. Here are some helpful hints:

■ It's worth the time and expense to hire a good bookkeeper who already works with real estate investors, and let that person set up your accounting correctly from the start.

- Use separate bank accounts for cash activity, which may include:
  Buying, holding, and renting
  Buying, fixing up, and selling
  Wholesaling properties
  Lease optioning
  Note brokering
  Partnering on properties
- Use one credit card for all business-related purchases that are tax-deductible for income tax purposes, and another for all personal expenses that are not tax-deductible.
- Each and every week and month, list all of your income, expenses, and projected cash needs, so you're not caught cashless. This also helps you prepare your financial statements and tax returns easily.
- Account for each property separately. Do not group houses together for accounting purposes.

Here's an idea that will add value: Sign up for a credit card that gives airline points for purchases charged on the card. Use this card to pay for your rehabilitation costs whenever possible. You might earn a free airline ticket (could be 20,000 or 30,000 points) for every property you fix up. When you close on the house and achieve your goal for it, take a trip with your free ticket. One month, I bought more than $80,000 in materials for repairs using my American Express card, which entitled me to two first-class airline tickets. Remember to pay off your card each month, and never borrow money you can't pay back.

Mistake # 62

Not Knowing Why You Are Really in Real Estate or What You Will Do with the Money You Make

The number-one factor in successful real estate investing (or in any endeavor) is *desire.* If you have enough desire, you will most likely accomplish everything and anything you want to do.

Write down the answer to this question: *Why are you in real estate?* Go ahead. Put this book down and do it now. Yes, stop reading and do it now. Okay—that's better. Are you in real estate to make more money? Achieve financial freedom? Be your own boss? Retire at a younger age than most? Have a better lifestyle? Buy a home? Pay for college for your children? Make a pile of cash so you can play and travel? Or is it for some greater purpose? Perhaps you want to spend more time with loved ones, family, and friends. Some of my most successful and dedicated students tap into a purpose that makes a difference for others. They want to make money to do charity work, to support their parents, to help their religious or spiritual institutions, to do healing work, to pursue passions such as travel, art, acting, or music.

Determine your *real* reason for wanting to become a successful, wealthy real estate investor. Write it down. Post the words on your desk and your mirror. Look at them every day. If your goal is to own a Ferrari, buy a toy one and put it on your desk to remind yourself every day. If you're working to take a special trip or pilgrimage, find posters of that special place and put them up in the rooms where you spend your time. Using these techniques, bring your ideas, dreams, and real motivations into reality.

Better yet, my office will send you a gift if you call 888-302-8018 and tell us your goals and motivations. Leave your name, number, address, and stated goals—whatever they are. You'll receive a free report worth $30 to remind you of those important goals.

When I started out, like many of you, I just wanted to be my own boss, take control of my time, and make a lot of money. Travel is one of my true passions, so I would make lots of deals and take a trip. Costa Rica, Germany, France, Greece, Egypt, Switzerland, Guatemala, California, New York, Cancun, Puerto Vallarta, Aruba, St. Martin, Venezuela, Sweden, Denmark, and Norway are all places I went in my first few years of real estate investing. Then my two major goals changed to these: to help others achieve success and to help homeless families become homeowners. In addition to these goals, I strive toward spiritual growth. All of these keep me excited and focused. What will keep you energized and motivated?

If you made $1 million from a real estate deal next month, what would you do? How would it change your life? How would you use it to affect others' lives? Would you donate some of it? How much? To whom?

Many of my students have become millionaires. All of them had a specific goal in mind—almost always one that focused on helping others. What are your goals?

Mistake # 63

Working Only on Making Big Deals When the Little Ones Pay the Bills

People love to tell you about the biggest and best deals they ever made. They talk about the home runs, grand slams, and really juicy real estate transactions that made them a fortune. Often, the novice (and sometimes the advanced) real estate investor focuses only on the really big deals.

There is nothing wrong with making big deals. However, you still have to keep the money coming in, the bills paid, and the family fed, which is generally accomplished by making a lot of small to medium-sized deals.

If you want to make a large deal, so be it. But be sure to allocate only a certain percentage of your time to those big elephants. Stay focused on what you are good at and what keeps the money flowing. I love to close big deals in the $2 million to $20 million range, but I'm still involved in a lot of houses in the $80,000 to $500,000 range.

I aim to spend only about 20 percent of my time on the larger, riskier deals or off-the-wall opportunities that come my way. You'll find that once you start making profitable real estate deals, all types of opportunities, schemes, and scams will come your way. Stay focused and do what you know well. My father once told me (and of course I didn't listen to him) that the most successful people stay *narrow* and *deep*. That is, do what you do best and keep doing it.

Anthony is a good friend of mine in life and in real estate. He reminded me of the mistake that we all have made or will make. He was wholesaling two to four houses a month in Nashville and making $8,000 to $20,00 on each house. Then he rolled his profits into one multimillion dollar deal. It was a good deal, but it took a long time to close, as many big deals do. Meanwhile, he stopped making the little deals that kept the cash coming in. He did well in the end, but it could have been disastrous. So be careful. Stay focused and keep doing what brings you success!

Mistake # 64

Thinking and Worrying Too Much, Then Losing the Deal

Confucius said, "He who hesitates is lost." Robert Shemin says, "Until you have a signed contract, you have nothing. And nothing has happened until certified funds have changed hands at closing."

Real estate investing is competitive. Many other investors are looking for motivated sellers. Therefore, if you find what looks like a good deal, then immediately get a signed contract or put an option on the property! So many investors have lost so many deals because they were "thinking about it." Don't think—take action! Find out:

- What the property is worth. Locate comparable sales and verify them with a market player—another investor or real estate agent who really knows the market.
- What the repairs will cost.
- What is the least amount the motivated seller will take.

Then write your offer and get a signed contract. This should be your number-one focus. Your number-two focus is to get it to closing, whether you are going to buy the property or wholesale it.

Every second counts when you're putting together a contract on a property. Fifteen minutes is a long time. Make the calls. Call the mortgage company, call the title company, and set up a closing. If you're going to sell or wholesale the property, call your potential buyers immediately. Set up a showing today or tomorrow—do not wait. Massive action creates massive results. Spend each and every minute of your working day focused on these two activities: contracting and closing. Breathe these words: *contract and close.* Don't get distracted. Ask yourself every 15 minutes: What action can I take now to expedite my goal to contract and close? Who can you call, e-mail, or fax to speed up the process?

Imagine: If you can make 20 calls an hour, and if you stayed focused for five hours a day, you could probably call about 100 people a day. What would happen if you did this for *10 weeks?* On the day before writing this, I made about 80 calls and found two deals in Miami. Last week, I personally responded to 150 For Rent ads, contacted 12 people, and set up two potentially great deals. One of them is a penthouse in South Beach, Florida.

How many contacts or offers can you get signed in the next 30 days? 60 days? 90 days? Go for it, and stay focused.

Mistake # 65

Not Understanding That Real Estate Investing Is a People Business

Most successful real estate investors have a few characteristics that are good to imitate. What do they do?

- They stick to what they set out to do.
- They keep an upbeat attitude.
- They use common sense.
- They keep it simple.
- They communicate clearly with others.

This doesn't mean that they're all outgoing, extravagant charmers. It means they understand that, like every business, real estate is a people business. To be successful, you'll have to learn to effectively deal with the following people:

- Motivated sellers who may be distressed
- Potential buyers
- Tenants
- Contractors
- Lenders
- Closing attorneys
- Escrow agents

- Bird dogs (people who can help you find deals)
- City officials (e.g., code enforcement officers)
- Other government officials, tax assessors, and the like

You need to develop good listening skills. The better you can understand what a person needs or wants, the better you're able to help that person. A good rule of thumb is to let others talk, then wait four to eight seconds until you're sure they've finished speaking before you respond. Instead of telling people what ideas will work, ask them what ideas they think will work. When they come up with the best ones, they'll feel a sense of ownership in these ideas.

Think about what you can do so that everyone will remember you in a positive light. My father taught me to give out candy, so whenever I visit my tenants, I give them and their children candy. It's dangerous to show up without it, because they all want the candy. Think about what you can do to cause people to remember you. More important, reward people who help you. What kind of unique gift can you give someone who has helped you in your real estate business?

Read books about successful people. Take classes from them. Study what they've done to become successful. From them, figure out how to improve the way you deal with people. The classes I've taken that have been most useful in real estate were in hypnosis, psychology, and handwriting analysis. Before I go into business with people, I examine their handwriting. Surprised? Think about it. Wouldn't it be helpful to know whether a potential real estate partner, assistant, property manager, contractor, or tenant is honest? Generally, if someone double-loops the o like this $\mathcal{O}$, they may be dishonest. Of course, you need a strong sample of a person's handwriting to draw conclusions, but it's good to be aware of handwriting traits that point to dishonesty and other undesirable possibilities.

What areas of interest would help *you* deal with people better?

Mistake # 66

Not Making a Real Commitment to Being a Successful Real Estate Investor

Most of us have tried different businesses and failed. We certainly know people who have tried and failed at real estate investing. Perhaps you have experimented with another kind of home-based business, network marketing, or a form of real estate. If you look at the people who have failed in these businesses, they all have one thing in common: *They did not stick with it.* If you look at all of the successful people in these businesses, they all have one common trait: *They all stuck with it.*

I can guarantee you one thing: You will be a much better, smarter real estate investor in your third year than in your first year! If you want to get better and make your investing business easier over time, just stick with it.

Start by making a minimum of a five-year commitment. Even if you set out to do it full time, run your business part-time for at least five years. Almost all of the investors who don't achieve anything make about a three-week commitment. If after this short amount of time, they don't make a lot of money, they quit. Then they jump to the next "opportunity" for about another three weeks.

Make a commitment—stick with it. In Year 2, it will be easier and better than in Year 1. If you stick with it for three years, you will be an expert. After five years, you will be a professional. Write down your commitment to making this business a success now:

_____

_____

_____

Mistake # 67

Not Having a Mentor or Coach

You know that any work that you do is a lot more fun and successful when you do it with someone else. In real estate investing, recruit someone who keeps you motivated, who helps you overcome mistakes, and who gives you another perspective on what you should or should not be doing. Most important, that mentor can help you see the big picture. When you have an experienced mentor or coach, your chances of success multiply tremendously.

Perhaps you can find a coach or mentor in your own community. Find older investors who are willing to help you. Offer to take them to lunch on a regular basis. If they assist you in finding a deal, work through a deal with you, or tell you how to make a deal better, reward them in some way. If you don't have a mentor or coach, call my office at 888-302-8018. We have a small coaching program that has helped both beginners and pros be successful much faster and more easily than if they were on their own. We have the capacity to work with only a few students at a time, so call to find out about openings.

For many years, I went to the gym to work out on my own. Sometimes I didn't feel like going and just wouldn't bother. Many times, I would go to the gym and spend half of the time socializing or hanging out at the water fountain. A few years ago, I hired a personal fitness coach. Now I always like going to the gym, because my trainer holds me responsible for showing up. He knows a lot about working out and saved me from making some big mistakes. I'm able to work out five times better with five times the results because I have a good coach.

The same principle holds true for students who work with the coaches in our coaching program: They get great results.

Mistake # 68

Missing Out on Lots of Deals and Thousands of Dollars Because You Stopped Following a Deal

Avoiding this mistake could potentially make you a truckload of money. Many times you call about a potential deal, go to a foreclosure, or look at a property, and you're told that it's been sold already, so you move on to the next deal. *Stop.* Don't do it! A potential deal is never over. Do more investigating. Find out who bought the property and what they're going to do with it. At the very least, you can add the buyer to your buyers list. Often the person who outbid you at an auction or beat you to a deal can become a good client. If the deal remains a good deal, perhaps you can pay that buyer something and still get the deal.

> For many years, I went to auctions of properties: tax sales, foreclosures, and regular auctions. I would set a price in my mind, and someone would almost always outbid me. I'd get frustrated, and I only purchased four properties after going to about 80 auctions over the course of three years. Then, one day, I asked the buyer who outbid me at a sale what he was going to do with the property. The house was worth about $85,000. It needed about $10,000 worth of repairs. I only wanted to pay about $45,000 for it. He bid and won it for $53,000. He told me that he wanted to wholesale it and make a few thousand dollars. I signed an option with him giving me the right to buy it for $56,000 anytime within the next 30 days. Then I wholesaled it to one of my buyers for $59,000 and made about $3,500 on a deal that I had initially lost. Furthermore, the gentleman who outbid me became a good real estate friend, and we have completed more than 15 deals together. That contact alone has generated more than $100,000 in profit for me.

Don't quit after you make an offer. Instead, follow the deal and find a pot of gold.

Here's another example. If you lose the opportunity to buy a property at a foreclosure or a short sale, call the new owner to see if a deal still exists. Meet the buyers and put them on your buyers list. Talk to them and find out what they are looking for, then locate that property *for* them, and earn a profit that way. Sellers, real estate agents, landlords, and property managers—you can work with them and for them, taking this never-stop approach further, and make a small fortune.

When you have a property for sale or rent, and someone calls who sounds interested but wants something different from what you have, maybe you typically respond by saying, "Sorry I can't help you." That's what I did for years. I would have a two-bedroom house for sale, and a caller would be asking for a three-bedroom. Or I'd have a place for rent in a decent neighborhood for $1,000 a month, but someone would call wanting an executive home in a great neighborhood for $2,000 a month. What did I do? I would turn that person away.

Not anymore. I take their names, qualify them over the phone, and find them what they want. It's a form of starting with the end buyer and working backward to the property.

Say you're running an ad to sell an $800,000 house. Some people see your ad or sign and call you, but can only afford a $600,000 home. Go find it for them. Use the lists and the network of other investors you have put together to locate what they want. Option the house from your investor friend for $560,000, and wholesale it to your buyer for $600,000. You make a profit by helping those you would have turned away before. Of course, it's always important to preapprove all buyers and tenants for their ability to pay.

Do the same with potential renters. If someone who sounds good (and easily goes through your prequalification system) wants to rent something you do not have, find it. Get a referral fee or set up a lease-option agreement so it will be a win-win situation.

John, a student of mine, got a call for a rental unit that he had just rented. The tenant sounded good and wanted to rent a place for $1,500 a month. John put together a one-year lease with a friend for $1,100 a month (his cost) with an option to buy it for $174,000. The place was worth about $200,000. John had the tenant preapproved. The tenant paid $6,000 up front and $1,500 a month for several months, then he bought the house for $200,000. John made a profit of $26,000 ($200,000 − $174,000 = $26,000 profit) plus the $6,000 down and $400 per month extra rent he collected for several months—from a call on a rental unit that was already rented. How many potential buyers, tenants, or lease optioners have you hung up on or passed by? What is the profit you could have made on those deals you walked away from? If you make one more deal, wholesale transfer, or lease option off of this one idea, how much would it be worth?

Here's the lesson: Never say never, and never say good-bye. Instead ask, "How can I help you? What are you looking for?"

Mistake # 69

Not Making Additional Income from Deals That You're Doing Anyway

Most people like you and me focus on only one or two ways to make money when they first get into real estate. For instance, you decide you are going to buy and rent a buy-fix-sell property. Nothing wrong with that. But now is the time to open your mind to new possibilities and increase your income by 30 to 50 percent (perhaps even 200 percent) without working too hard.

Look at what other businesses do and how they make their money. For example, when you buy a car from a dealership, the dealership makes a lot of its money not just from selling you a car but also by offering you extras:

- Financing warranties
- Servicing
- Insurance
- Add-ons like extra body coatings and upgrades

In your business, like theirs, once you've done the hard part—finding the client—consider what else you can easily offer your customers that will benefit them and bring in more profits for you. Think for a moment: If you are selling houses by fixing them up, what else might your sellers and buyers need? They'd be looking for extras such as these:

- Financing
- Insurance

- Closing services
- Maintenance, repairs, and upgrades
- Appliances
- Legal insurance
- Consulting services
- Security alarms
- Real estate brokerage services

Without losing focus on your primary business, you may want to spend some time and find the *best* providers of these services in your area. Then work out a referral program in writing. Perhaps a 10 to 20 percent referral fee off what the service provider makes is appropriate. Remember, you're bringing customers they would not have acquired otherwise.

If you cannot work out a good referral program that will pay you, at least trade services. That is, perhaps you can refer business to service providers, and they can perform services for you. Real estate agents are generally not allowed to pay referral fees or commissions except to other licensed agents. Therefore, many large real estate companies have affiliated with or even purchased mortgage companies, title companies, and insurance brokerages. In partnership with them, not only will you make your normal profit, but you could make the following:

You sell a $200,000 home. The mortgage participation fee is 2 points ($4,000).	
You get 30 percent of the points for helping to originate the mortgage.	$1,200
You get 20 percent of the title closing fees ($1,500).	$300
You get your portion of the title insurance and fee.	$300
You sell a Pre-Paid Legal plan; you get a commission.	$100
You refer a contractor to do a $10,000 upgrade; you make 10 percent.	$1,000

You could make an extra $2,900 off this deal. How many deals are you going to do? How long will you be in the business?

I know that you could use some extra cash flow. So please consider what your tenants could use and how you can help them. Many large apartment and management companies profit by asking their tenants what items they want or need, then going and finding them. If you make an extra 5 to 25 percent of what your tenants are going to spend anyway, it will help them and increase your bottom line.

If you are going to develop these additional areas of income, make sure you do the following:

- Find the best, highest quality providers of goods and services. Be sure to test them out yourself before you make any referrals.
- Make all arrangements and agreements in writing. Clearly define the terms and time of payments.
- Disclose in writing to your customers that you don't guarantee or warranty any of your vendors, and disclose to them that you may be paid for referring them to vendors. Have your customers sign these disclosures.

Be sure to keep an open mind, and don't overlook the opportunity to make an extra $500 to $5,000 a month. Many months, I get an extra $1,000 to $3,000 from these simple referral fees. The best part is that my clients, buyers, sellers, and tenants appreciate the high-quality referrals I send their way. If you're interested in looking into affiliating with a mortgage company or Pre-Paid Legal Services, call my office at 888-302-8018 for complete details.

Mistake # 70

Not Focusing on the Activities That Will Make Money for You Today

It's important to make plans and set goals, but the most important plans, goals, and thoughts you can have include these questions:

What am I going to do—
    Now?
    Today?
    This week?
    This month?
    This quarter?
—To get good deals and make money *now!*

Create a detailed daily action plan to get your business going now. You already know what makes you the most money and is the most enjoyable activity for you. Generally, it's finding the deal and putting it together. How are you going to find good deals today? This week? This month?

Here is an action plan that I recommend for both beginners and pros. This action plan is based on a six- to eight-hour workweek. If you follow it, you will learn a lot, meet a lot of good contacts, and most likely start to develop the following:

- Sources for motivated sellers and their deals
- Buyers of property
- Sources of funds to buy and close investment property

Start each day by writing down your goals. Then, at the end of the day, be sure to review them and set plans for the following day.

Week 1

■ Call 20 For Sale by Owner ads, Investment Property ads, I Buy Houses ads and For Rent ads. You can probably make 20 calls in less than an hour. The hardest part of real estate investing, as in most businesses, is contacting people.

■ Pick an area that is in transition. Drive for dollars for one or two hours. Hunt down all For Sale by Owner homes, For Rent signs, vacant homes—in general, homes that need work. Get a real estate agent to look up the owners of the homes (or do it yourself). Call the ads and owners, or send them a letter saying, "I want to buy your house. If you are interested in talking, call me at xxx-xxxx."

■ Call six finance companies and ask whether they have any foreclosure properties on their books right now. Ask to speak to the manager of the foreclosures department, and be persistent until you get to speak directly to that person.

Week 2

■ Call four auction companies. Get on their mailing lists and ask them if they ever know of any deals that don't go to auction. Remember, you are always building a buyers list, sellers list, and financial resources list. Go to a few auctions and build your buyers list by talking to other investors who attend. Remember, if they buy at auction, they are cash buyers. Get to know at least three real buyers at the auction. Ask them what they are looking for, and go find it for them.

■ Invite one experienced investor to lunch. Do this every week. Ask those who join you about their businesses and what kind of deals they're looking for. Do they have anything to sell? Would they fund a great deal that you might find?

■ Call 20 For Rent ads looking for motivated sellers or lease-option candidates.

Week 3

■ Find and join your local real estate investors association. (Call my office at 888-302-8018 to help you locate one in your area.) Make a point of becoming active in your local group. Many of the most successful investors become volunteers with their real estate investment club. When you volunteer for these associations, you will meet a lot of people and probably will also make a lot of deals as a result of knowing them.

■ Make five offers on five properties. Even if you have not found a really motivated seller yet, just shoot out five low offers that include your contingency clause so you assume no risk. This will help you get over the block of making offers. Some of my most successful students simply make a lot of offers—50 to 100 a week. Like any business, real estate investing is a numbers game.

■ Drive for dollars in the neighborhoods where you're interested in buying properties and find some good prospects.

Week 4

■ Find out about foreclosure sales, tax-lien sales, or sheriff's sales and go to them. To find them, call the property tax office, look for foreclosure listings in your paper, and just meet other interested investors there when you attend.

■ Find five *bird dogs*—people who can help you find deals. They can be other investors, repair people, delivery people, police officers, utility workers, real estate agents, and others. Ask them to spot properties that could be candidates for sale and contact you.

If you continue these activities for several weeks, you will soon be making offers and well on your way to closing deals. Remember, it's the basic activities that make you money in real estate. Keep calling, keep meeting people, and keep focusing on the activities that will make your real estate investment business profitable.

Mistake # 71

Letting Your Emotions Rule Your Choice of Rehab Projects Instead of Analyzing the Numbers

When you're doing the analysis on a potential rehab property, make it a rule of thumb that if you have triple-checked your projected expenses and calculated that you'll net less than a 40 percent return, you'll stop right there. Let your decision to buy this property be ruled by logic and numbers, not your personal feelings about it.

Suppose you buy a rehab house for $62,000. Its estimated repair expenses are $22,000, and holding costs are $6,000, for a grand total of $90,000. You had better be able to sell the property for at least $150,000 net—a minimum of 40 percent return on your investment. I recommend building in at least a 40 percent cushion of safety to cover these possible circumstances: The contractor takes a much longer time getting the job completed, your property doesn't sell for a year or more, your buyers cannot qualify for a loan, or you have to deal with unforeseen repairs, extra holding costs, and so forth.

Keep in mind that more than 50 percent of rehab projects lose money. Don't be a victim of those statistics; follow the 40 percent rule.

Mistake # 72

Overrehabbing a Property

A trick of the trade I've learned from pros who have piled up fortunes is this: Don't overspend on your rehab projects. That's how many sellers get into deep water.

In an effort to glamorize a property, it's easy to go overboard and spend far too much on upgrades and renovations, thinking this will increase the value of the property and make it easier to sell. Too often, rehabbers want the place to look immaculate—everything to be perfect and to their own taste. But they forget that their prospects might be looking for different things than they would look for themselves.

Bathrooms and kitchens are important to the sale of a home, but that doesn't mean you have to spend a fortune on cabinets or vanities. It's better to maximize your profits by putting in basic, clean items that work. Adding some brass, a bit of landscaping, a few ceiling fans, and the like can make a difference in selling or renting a property. But if the remodeling costs put the house at the wrong price for the market—no matter how great it looks—it won't make you the profits you want.

The point is this: You have to determine what it will take to motivate someone to buy your property in today's market, without putting you in a bind. Be aware that every dollar you spend can elevate the price of the property, perhaps even above its current market value. Find out what the standards are in the neighborhood and conform to those.

Mistake # 73

Not Finding Out the Underlying Reasons Why People Are Selling Their Properties

This is the secret to success: Give people what they want. A skilled, compassionate investor learns how to probe and find out the real reasons.

A few years ago, I found a newspaper ad listing eight houses for sale. The ad said, "Owner financing possible. Call xxx-xxxx." I phoned the seller and asked lots of questions: Where are the properties, how much do they rent for, what kind of financing was he offering, and so on. He was offering 20 percent down, with a note for 20 years at 8 percent interest. I looked at the eight houses, which included two duplexes, some single-family homes, and two homes with a large tract of land. They were in good shape, all rented, and with proper cash coming in. It seemed to be a good deal at first.

I met the seller for lunch and asked 1,000 more questions. In my mind, I was happy to offer the price he was asking, knowing that many others were interested in buying the properties. He questioned me, too, and grew comfortable regarding my ability to actually close on the deal and manage the properties well so he wouldn't have to take them back—a big fear among sellers offering owner's terms.

During our discussion, it became apparent *why* he was selling the properties. He had inherited them through an estate settlement, he didn't enjoy managing them, he had another job that took up a lot of his time, and he didn't want to be worrying about them. However, the key reason why he wanted to sell was that the debt on the property equaled $50,000, and a note on the property required a payment of $1,088 every month.

When I uncovered this information, I offered him exactly what he wanted: to take over the note and give him the exact amount of money he needed to pay off the debt. The end result: I got the property at a much lower price than I had originally anticipated, just by finding out what he really needed.

Mistake # 74

Getting Too Greedy When Flipping to Other Investors

If you know you've found a great deal, sell it quickly for a medium to high profit. The likelihood of selling the home to another investor for a big payoff is small; it's more likely that you'll gain a reputation as someone who tries to overprice deals. That's not a reputation you want, because nobody will choose to do business with you.

> The key is high volume and medium profits. You can't look at the wholesaling business as a one-time short. When you sell property to other investors, you want them to make a profit, too. And you want them to be happy with the deal. Make friends in this business by making sure others profit as well.

Mistake # 75

Not Being Generous with Your Partners and Coinvestors

My rule is to always pay partners and coinvestors more than they expect. Why? You're after repeat business, not a one-time killing.

Look at this from the investors' viewpoint. If you promise the investors 10 percent on their money and then pay them 11 or 12 percent—explaining that you made so much money on this deal that you wanted to share it—do you think they'll want to do business with you again? Of course! Repeat business is what you're after. If you flip or rehab a property and make $15,000, then once you sell it, give your investor an extra $1,000 after your agreed-upon split. Say it's a bonus for working with you. Chances are that investor will be so pleased, he or she will tell friends, relatives, and business partners that you're a good person to lend money to in the future.

PART II

Three Bonus Mistakes

Mistake # 76

Not Knowing to Ask for Owner's Terms

It's wise to always ask for owner's terms. And it's possible to get them if you apply your best negotiation skills.

Almost all sellers will say they want cash as payment for a sale of property. If they demand cash, ask them why. Usually, they will tell you their plans for the cash—paying off a debt, for example. You respond by asking the sellers what they will do with the rest of the money once the debt is paid off. They might say they can earn 4 to 6 percent on their money. You respond by asking, "How would you like to pay off your debt and earn more interest with a very safe investment?" You've piqued their interest because it surpasses their expectations while meeting their needs. Then you offer them $3,000 cash down with owner's terms for the balance over 20 or 30 years at a rate of interest higher than 6 percent. Chances are you'll get a better deal this way, and the sellers can earn more interest on their money over time.

Mistake # 77

Failing to Aggressively Market Properties You Have for Sale

Develop an active, ongoing, action-oriented marketing plan that includes advertising, direct mail, telemarketing, seminars, and counseling services.

Experiment with different ads, letters, and telemarketing strategies. Your goal is not necessarily the number of prospects that respond, but rather how many properties you actually close on. If you spend $60 every week on mailings to 100 people, and you get a 2 percent response, you will generate 20 new prospects in every 10-week period. How many will you turn into buyers?

Mistake # 78

Not Giving People More Than They Expect

Always give people, family, friends, tenants, and real estate clients more than they expect. Most people overpromise and underdeliver. Make it your guiding business principle to underpromise and overdeliver.

This book promises 75 mistakes and delivers more, plus extras on how to find great deals and a list of the Top-10 Real Estate Mistakes We Make Every Day, which you should work with daily. (See appendixes.)

I recommend always rewarding good work and providing more value for the same money. That way, people appreciate you and want to continue to do business with you. For example, I give my contractors a bonus if they do great work. Sometimes, if an investor makes a deal happen, I send extra money or a certificate for a nice dinner out, or I'll pay for a free trip. It's fun to do; it's the right thing to do. If you do it, too, you'll find it will increase your business and profits.

Happy investing, and may your success as an investor be 10 times greater than you ever expected!

Almost Every Possible Way
to Find Great Deals

The lesson is simple: If you cannot find great deals in real estate, you cannot make much money. This bonus chapter features 46 avenues for finding deals.

What Is a Great Deal?

Say a friend of yours is getting divorced, has to move away, needs cash quickly, and says, "I have this Jaguar worth about $50,000. It's in great shape. If I could just get $30,000 for it, I'd be okay." The car was brand-new the year before, purchased for about $55,000.

How could you make money off that Jaguar? You could call dealers, who are wholesalers, and ask, "What is a 2001 Jaguar worth today?"

They'd reply, "About $50,000." So you'd ask, "What would you pay for it?" and they'd say, "We'd have to make something on the resale, so we'd pay $42,000 for it."

If the dealership gives you $42,000, and you give your friend $30,000, you would make $12,000. Alternatively, you could run an ad in the newspaper offering the Jaguar for, say, $45,000. You would make even more money. Or you could take $30,000 from your savings or borrow it from a bank, lease the Jaguar for $600 a month, and bring in money every month that way.

You have similar choices in real estate, too, but first you have to find a deal like the one your friend with the Jaguar handed you. If you find a good deal, you will make good money. If you find a great deal, you will make great money.

What Is One Deal Worth?

What if you find one great deal—a house you can buy and hold? You borrow $100,000, rent the house out, and pay for it in 15 years. By then, it's worth $300,000, and you have made thousands on it.

Or what if you find another great deal—a house you can turn over, flip, or wholesale? You make between $8,000 and $20,000 in a short time by selling it shortly after you buy it.

What if you lease-option a house? With this method, you get three pay-days. The tenants pay you up front with option money. You lease the house out every month and have $300 to $500 extra cash flow coming in. And when they actually buy the house, you make another $15,000.

Returns like these are possible with good and great deals. If you are not searching out these deals, you could be wasting your time in real estate.

Finding Motivated Sellers

To find good deals, find motivated sellers. If a property is worth $100,000 in the marketplace, and the seller wants $99,000 for it, the seller simply is not hungry to sell. What motivates some people to sell at below-market prices, and how can you identify them?

Here are some indicators for identifying highly motivated sellers:

- Poor health
- Recent divorce
- Recent unemployment
- Estate sale due to death
- Relocation or adoption of a new lifestyle

Sometimes people face a health crisis, a divorce, or the death of a loved one. They lose their jobs or their desire to care for their property. In the turmoil of these transitions, they have difficulty paying their expenses, including their mortgages. Although the circumstances may be sad, if you can help them avoid foreclosure on their property by getting cash into their hands, you have provided an important service.

Please understand that I am *not* saying that you should take advantage of people or rip them off. If you ever have a transaction in which *every* party is not *completely* satisfied with the deal, *move on*.

The following ideas generate good deals for many investors, and they can work for you, too. They are listed under these categories: Newspaper Ads, Driving for Dollars, Advertising, Networking, Bird Dogging, Courts, Foreclosures, and Special Sales.

Newspaper Ads

Reading newspaper ads at least every Sunday or more often will get you started. If you follow sports, you read the Sunday paper religiously. You learn about the heights and weights of the athletes, their playing statistics, even their arrest records in some cases. If you study the real estate section in the same way, you will become an expert in real estate just as you are in sports. It's similar to how some people follow stocks. They know every detail about them and watch their movements 15 times a day. If you did one-tenth of that activity in real estate by steadily going through the real estate section every week, you would become an expert in real estate.

When you read the newspaper, what are you looking for? Suspects—highly motivated sellers who become prospects. The following 10 ideas suggest where to look to get started.

Suggestion # 1:   For Rent Ads

If a property is for rent, it's often empty, and the owners are paying a mortgage on it but are not collecting rent. The landlord or management company may be tired of renting it out and keeping it repaired. Sometimes you can get a great deal and help them get out of the business altogether.

Suggestion # 2:   For Sale by Owner Ads

If people are selling their houses by themselves, that might mean they cannot afford a real estate agent or are in a hurry to sell.

Suggestion # 3:   For Sale Ads

Look at For Sale ads to quickly learn what property sells for in specific neighborhoods. Search for such phrases as *Must Sell, Make Offer,* and *Won't Last.* I circle those ads and call to find suspects who might become prospects.

In the process of calling, you will learn which real estate agents are active in which areas. Get to know them, because if you ever find a deal in their territory, they could help you locate buyers or sellers.

Suggestion # 4:   Investment Property Ads

These ads generally mean that an investor or landlord either purchased a property years ago and wants the profits from the appreciation in value, or bought a bad deal and is tired of dealing with the property. In either case, the owner or landlord could be highly motivated to sell.

I like to start with these properties because they are being sold by other investors, who are burned out and motivated to sell. I can also add these contacts to the lists I'm constantly building: my lists of buyers, sellers, and sources of funds. Remember, 80 to 90 percent of my deals are with other investors.

When I call, I always ask, "Do you have or know of any other properties for sale?" I recommend that you always ask that question when you call. Here is why.

I once responded to an ad from this section, and the older gentleman who answered said, "I've got this property and I'm selling it at 30 percent below what it's worth. I'll do owner's terms. I have pictures of it, and I really want to sell, so I'll be more than glad to work with you."

Then I asked that important question: "Do you have any others?"

He said, "I'm so glad you asked. I've got 88 more, all with pictures and documentation."

I ended up buying all of them and flipped about 50 in about a year.

Suggestion # 5:   Lease-Option Ads

Check for a Lease Option section in your paper. Investors looking for deals or putting deals together usually place ads here. Remember, they are investors. And if you are also an investor who is going to be wholesaling, you not only want deals that you can buy, you want people you can sell to. Always get their names, addresses, phone numbers, fax numbers, e-mail addresses, and information on what type of property they like. Also ask, "Do you know of any good sources of financing?" Build your lists of people who can get you money as well as get you deals.

Every time you talk to an investor, you are looking for three things:

- A deal you can buy
- A deal of yours that they can buy
- Good sources of financing

Suggestion # 6:   Auction Ads

Auctions, listed in the back of the real estate section, are becoming a popular way to sell property. Some estimate that over the next five years, about 40 to 50 percent of all property may be auctioned.

Auction companies advertise, conduct the auction, sell the property, and close the deal 10 to 30 days later. If they have properties they cannot auction, they sell them at a discount, because auctioneers are always finding motivated sellers who want to offload their properties quickly.

When you go to real estate auctions, whom do you meet? Buyers who have cash. (Some deals offer owner's terms or financing, but many require cash.) Go to an auction as if it were a cocktail party. Meet everybody there and build your buyers list. Get names, addresses, phone numbers, fax numbers, and e-mail addresses. These investors find deals that they could pass on to you and vice versa. All the while, you keep your eyes open for a great deal.

Suggestion # 7:   Legal Notices

You will find legal notices in many newspapers. They announce bank-ruptcies, divorces, foreclosures, and estate sales. You might find highly motivated sellers in any one of these areas, plus you can find a lot of great deals and work with your attorney on the technical details. These deals can be worth the effort.

Every major city has a legal newspaper. Call a local attorney or go down to a magazine shop, find out the name, and buy it. It is full of listings of foreclosures, tax liens, bankruptcies, estate sales, and divorces. You do not have to understand the legal mumbo jumbo. Simply call the attorney listed or get an address off the legal notice and send a letter asking about the possibility of a deal.

Suggestion # 8:   Obituaries

If you read an obituary in the newspaper, what does that mean to you? The deceased usually leaves behind real estate, furniture, cars, and often widely dispersed family members. You could be doing the relatives a ser-vice by writing or calling them and saying, "I am so sorry to hear about your loss, but if you have any property you want to dispose of quickly, I can help you. I might be interested in taking it over." In a lot of instances, people say, "We don't want to deal with this house. The children and cousins have moved across the country. Just take the house; you're doing us a favor. Yes, we know we're selling way below what it's worth, but we don't have time to deal with it. Too many memories. Just take it."

I've been teaching this method for years, and one of my students has been extremely successful at it. He responds to all the obituaries in writing and usually gets 10 to 20 deals a year in a very small town. Many times, the people write him a letter thanking him after he has put the property under contract, fixed it up, and sold it. They say, "Thank you so much for taking that property off our hands. We didn't want to have to deal with everything." Sometimes he not only gets the house, but also acquires cars, furniture, and collectibles.

Suggestion # 9: Neighborhood Newspapers

Some of the best deals can be found in the *Thrifty Nickel,* the *Shopper's News,* and other neighborhood papers, because people who place ads

---

Following Up on a "Must Sell" Ad

A student of mine, Don, saw a Must Sell ad in the newspaper for a commercial property in Miami, Florida. He did not know much about Miami, but he called the broker listed in the ad and asked this critical question: "Why is this being sold?"

The broker replied, "The woman is selling because her husband was the landlord. He just passed away and she doesn't want to manage it. She's tired of it. She wants to dump it. The building is worth as much as $1.4 million but it needs $200,000 of work. She'd take $500,000 for it."

Don offered a lot less than that and got the building under contract for $290,000. He wants to wholesale it and stands to make $100,000 to $300,000. The end buyer will also get a great deal, because Don is asking $700,000 to $800,000 for this $1.4 million building.

Who wins? Everybody. The widow is happy to let go of the property after making money with it over the past 30 years. The broker will make a good commission; Don will see a large profit; the end buyer will get an incredible deal. And it all started from calling an ad in the local newspaper.

---

there cannot afford to advertise in the big daily paper. I have experimented and found that if you have $200 to spend on advertising, you will likely get better results from advertising in the smaller papers. Not only are they good sources for finding deals, but you also get more bang for your advertising buck. (More about advertising later in this appendix.)

Suggestion # 10:   Legal Newspapers

Deals such as foreclosures are generally listed in the community's legal newspaper. In most cities and counties, they must be advertised in the legal or regular papers a few weeks before the sale occurs.

Driving for Dollars

Doesn't this sound like the name of a game show? "Good evening, ladies and gentlemen. In tonight's edition of *Driving for Dollars,* we have two contestants." But you can make a lot of money at this game, which is my favorite source of finding good deals. It's fun to go with someone who will write down the addresses as you find promising properties.

Pick a neighborhood that you are interested in—one in transition, being fixed up, has houses that need work, and so on. Drive around it slowly, and try to find at least 20 addresses of neglected, vacant, or condemned homes, ones with signs saying For Sale, For Sale by Owner, or For Rent.

Be persistent. You may have to call and call and call to find the owners. Start by calling the registrar of deeds, logging onto web sites on the Internet, and going to the local tax records office to locate the owners.

Ask a real estate agent to look them up on the multiple-listing service computer. Then call or write the owners once you find them.

As you drive neighborhoods, learning about them and looking for "suspects" (potential motivated sellers), make a point of meeting the agents and brokers who are active in that area. You will learn a tremendous amount from talking with them.

Suggestion # 11: Driving for Dollars and Looking for Landmarks

Look for the following landmarks and clues:

- *Neglect.* Look for gutters that hang, roofs with holes in them, and horrible-looking yards with trash lying everywhere. The worse the disrepair, the better the deal. The more work the house needs, the more motivated the seller will be. The more motivated the seller, the better the deal will be.

- *Undeveloped land.* Look for land on the edge of town; write a letter and find the owner.

- *Vacant homes.* The house is empty, the grass is high, the bushes are overgrown, and the place looks deserted—could those sellers be motivated? Absolutely. Put them on your suspects' list.

- *Condemned homes.* Look for that yellow tape that says, "Unfit for human habitation." This signifies a code violation that's exciting for investors, because owners who have already been to court might be highly motivated to sell. The codes enforcement section of the local housing administration has fined them. The fines are equivalent to saying, "If you do not fix this house, we will fine you more, and if you still don't fix it by a certain time, we will bulldoze your property."

Diamond in the Rough

The best deal my friend John ever got involved in was a house that had 35 feet of garbage in the front yard. Drug addicts had lived in the place. When he walked into the house, he could not even get access to the basement because of the garbage.

But the real estate market was hot in this neighborhood, and 50 people looked at the house during its first two days on the market. Everyone who saw it walked away in disgust. Most people insist on buying a house that looks like a new present with a bow on it.

John went into the trashed-out house, took a big breath in the smelly environment, and declared, "Ah, Paradise. Eureka. The mother lode." He figured that the house was worth about $350,000 fixed up. He determined that it needed about $50,000 worth of repairs, so he put it under contract for $140,000 (less than half of its value) and got the deal done. This example proves my point: The worse the house, the better the deal.

- *For Rent signs.*   If a house is for rent, you might find a highly motivated landlord who bought the property 20 years ago for a fifth of what it is now worth and is tired of it. The best ones are the empty ones. Call on these, too.

- *For Sale and For Sale by Owner signs.*   These signs might say "Make Offer," so pay close attention.

Advertising

In my experience, if you do not advertise, nothing will happen. And if you do advertise, something *will* happen.

Suggestion # 12:   Business Cards

Make your business card stand out by printing your information on shocking-bright card stock. The wording on your card should get people's attention and tell them what you can do for them. "We will pay cash for your house. Can close quickly. Call me first. Call me last." You might include such wording as, "If you are in trouble through foreclosure, bankruptcy, divorce, need to raise cash, need to raise money, need to sell your property quickly, call me now." Put your cell phone number on the card in a prominent place. Hand out your cards to everybody.

Suggestion # 13:   Advertising Flyers

Make flyers—and distribute lots of them. The flyers might say, "We will pay cash for your house. Can close quickly. Call me first. We will buy your house. We will make an offer on every property." You want your phone to ring so you can find great deals.

Suggestion # 14:   Your Own Ads in Local Papers

Place an ad in your local newspaper that states, "We will buy houses. We will pay cash." Typically, these ads generate two to three calls a day and lead to about one deal a week. Is that worth $190 a week to run an ad? Yes, because one deal can be worth a lot.

Run your ad consistently and for a long time. This is critical. If you run it for three months to a year and the wording attracts attention, you will get calls and, eventually, good deals.

Suggestion # 15:   Direct-Mail Campaigns

Sending direct mail through the postal service usually gets a response rate of 1 to 2 percent, so do not expect a high-volume return for your efforts. But if you mail a large quantity, you will get activity. Monitor the numbers carefully, and be consistent in your direct-mail campaign, so you know what works well for you.

Suggestion # 16:   Door Hangers

When you come home at night, sometimes you see advertisements for carpet cleaning and pizza specials hanging on your door. You can use this idea and pay the same people to hand out your door hangers. Your message would read: "We pay cash for a house. Can close quickly. Do you know of any houses for sale that are a good deal? Call me. Referral fees paid."

Suggestion # 17:   Co-op Advertising

You can partner with businesses that are already advertising through flyers, door hangers, even pizza boxes. Instead of advertising alone, you combine your efforts with others and spread your message farther for the same amount of money and time spent.

Think about all the people advertising on restaurant menus, on shopping carts, on street signs in your targeted neighborhoods. If you can cooperate with any of them, you will generate calls that can lead to good deals.

Suggestion # 18:   Signs

Put signs on every corner in your targeted neighborhood, and you will get calls. The largest real estate franchises attract prospects by running billboards that say, "We will buy any house, ugly or pretty. We will pay cash. Call now." These signs generate lots of calls, and the companies make lots of money.

Suggestion # 19:   Car Signs

I once flew to Ohio to speak at a real estate association. I noticed that the fellow who picked me up at the airport had put a big plastic sign on the side of his Jeep Cherokee that said, "We will pay cash for your house. Call me." I thought, "I don't like the way this ugly sign covers up a beautiful truck." But I asked Dennis if he got calls from this sign. He replied, "I get about five calls a week and one deal a month. I made about $8,000 on one of them last month and $25,000 on a fixer-upper." That ugly sign becomes a beautiful one when motivated sellers call you.

Everywhere a Sign

An investor named John in Ohio owns more than 900 houses. Why does he have 900 houses while you and I do not? Because he places signs on park benches, on street corners, and on pizza boxes. He prints and distributes flyers, door hangers, and business cards. This kind of advertising works where John lives, and it will work where you live, too.

Networking

Investing is a lonely business. Go meet other people, talk to them, and help each other out. Here are some categories of people who can refer good deals to you.

Suggestion # 20:   Real Estate Agents

Real estate agents have access to the multiple-listing service and to buyers and sellers. Get to know the active agents in your targeted areas. When good deals come their way, they will call someone, and that someone should be you. Make sure they get paid when they find deals so you keep your relationships golden. By the way, if I use agents and brokers but do not close on a property with them, I always give them a check for their time until they find me something. It keeps the relationship solid.

Suggestion # 21:   Attorneys

In every area, a couple of top law firms handle most of the foreclosures and bankruptcies. Get to know the people in those firms and work with them. Understand that they care about client confidentiality, so they cannot tell you certain things, but they do know about pending deals. They will call somebody about them, so it might as well be you. Attorneys can do a lot to help your business. Find several active attorneys in your area and network with them.

Suggestion # 22: CPAs, Accountants, and Bookkeepers

When people want to do financial planning, settle their estate, sell some property, raise money, or get out of financial trouble, they turn to their trusted accountant or financial planner. These professionals often help clients dispose of their property, so get to know them and include them in your network.

Suggestion # 23: Bankers and Mortgage Brokers

Bankers and brokers make loans to real estate people and often know where good deals are. Because they have access to funds, they might finance the good deals you find. They also know lots of other investors and can help you expand your network.

Suggestion # 24: Local Real Estate Investors Associations

These groups can be a gold mine for finding like-minded investors you can partner with. Check at www.sheminrealestate.com for a list of associations around the country.

Bird Dogging

Bird dogs are the white dogs with brown spots that flush out rabbits and quail for hunters. In real estate, *bird dogs* are people who can flush out deals for you.

Most successful businesses rely on many people to get things done, and everyone in the organization benefits. It is hard to be a lone wolf in the investing business; you can only look at so many deals, drive around so many neighborhoods, write so many letters, and make so many phone calls yourself. I pay my bird dogs $500 to $1,000 for bringing a deal to me. I find 20 to 30 percent of my deals this way.

Who can act as your bird dogs to spot good deals for you? Everyone you know—because everyone knows someone who has to sell a property at a discount or is dealing with an estate, getting a divorce, having money problems, going into bankruptcy, and so on.

Following are several categories of people who can be your bird dogs.

Suggestion # 25:   Contractors

Every contractor, big or small, is going out and looking at properties that need work. Contractors know owners, and some of those owners will be motivated to sell. Contact every contractor and repair person you know and say, "If you bring me a deal that I close on, I will pay you a finder's fee."

Suggestion # 26:   Utility Workers

Utility workers—from the gas company, electric company, water company—are out walking and driving neighborhoods every day. They know a lot about houses, neighborhoods, and the people they deal with. They may be able to say, "Hey, I know about a house that needs a lot of work. We shut the service off. And here's the owner's name and the address." They can be your bird dogs.

Suggestion # 27:   Postal Workers

Often postal workers know more about you and your neighbors than you think they do. They know who is getting divorced, who is moving, who has to sell a house. In fact, some successful real estate investors are postal workers. Ask them to help you identify good deals.

Suggestion # 28:   Police Officers

Police officers have a tough job in the neighborhoods. They get to know about houses or properties that can be sold, especially ones they've just locked up because somebody did something illegal there. They can point you to motivated sellers.

Suggestion # 29:   Nursing Home Workers

Our population is getting older, and more people are moving into retirement, assisted living, and nursing homes. Often, people are forced to sell their property and their assets to qualify for financial assistance before going into a home.

One of my students visits nursing homes to find good deals. He makes friends with the administrators, who call him and say, "Mrs. Smith has to sell her home, and the family doesn't want to deal with it. Can you help them out?" He gets a lot of good deals that way. He's not taking advantage of the situation; he truly is helping them. And he discloses in writing exactly what he is doing.

Suggestion # 30:   Retail Finance Companies

Located in malls and shopping centers, these companies make high-risk loans to high-risk borrowers. Look them up in the Yellow Pages under "Finance Companies." Their names include Associates, Beneficial, and American General. They make all kinds of loans, but also lend money to people who may not have perfect credit. Some have local, regional, or national foreclosure centers where you can call about properties available. Often, they will sell them for the outstanding amount of the loan.

Suggestion # 31:   Letter Writing and Follow-up

Whenever I send a letter to a prospect, I always follow up with a phone call. That alone triples my response rate. Write first, then call and ask

In Times of Desperation

I once attended a seminar where I learned some information that I will pass on to you, saving you lots of time learning it for yourself. It is this: When people get into financial trouble—heading for bankruptcy or foreclosure—they follow a predictable pattern of behavior. They run to their accountants, mortgage brokers, and financial planners. In desperation, they may call a real estate agent and say, "Can you sell my house in three weeks?" As a last resort, they call a bankruptcy attorney.

Because of this pattern, you want to build a network of mortgage bankers, real estate agents, attorneys, and accountants, so that when desperate people call them, they will send those callers to you. You can pay the sellers cash for their house, turn it over quickly, make money for yourself, and possibly prevent them from going bankrupt.

such questions as, "How long have you had the property? Would you be interested in selling? Can I help out?"

Suggestion # 32:   Real Estate Associations

Most major cities have a real estate association and a landlords association. Who attends? Investors, landlords, and people who know how to find good deals. Associations are great sources of education, too. At www.sheminrealestate.com, we provide a list of real estate associations. Network at the meetings, and you will find everything you need to become a successful real estate investor.

Courts

Some real estate investors always complain about the government—the IRS, courts, regulations. But I love the government. As a real estate investor, you should love the government, too, because it is hard at work producing hundreds of thousands of motivated sellers. All types of courts exist to help create motivated sellers (even when the sellers don't think they're being motivated). Here are some of them.

Suggestion # 33:   Codes Court

Go down to your local housing administration office to learn the scheduled dates for codes court where landlords and investors go to defend their interests. The codes court enforces the codes and can issue fines. It can even condemn homes and have them bulldozed. Do motivated sellers come to these courtrooms? Yes.

The proceedings are all a matter of public record. The docket for the day is usually posted outside the courthouse. You can talk to the people while they are there, and meet with the lawyers, landlords, and investors who attend. When I go to codes court, I usually find a good deal. Chances are you will, too.

Suggestion # 34:   Eviction Court

In every major city, eviction court meets at least a few days a week. Who shows up there? Tenants, attorneys, landlords, and managers. Owners who have a conflict on their hands and go to court to resolve it could be in the market to sell for a good price.

Know that when you go to eviction court, you may find some great deals, and you will definitely find better entertainment than anything on television. You will also network with people you want to know. And if you do not want to spend time there, you can get names, addresses, and phone numbers of people on the docket. Send them a letter asking, "Do you have any properties you'd like to sell?" and follow up.

Suggestion # 35:   Environmental Court

People who have too much junk on their properties wind up in environmental court. The court fines people for not removing trash and not cleaning their yards. Owners of these properties can be highly motivated to sell. Go meet them, get their names, and contact them afterward. They could be sources of good deals.

Suggestion # 36:   Divorce Court

Because divorce records are public, you can actually look up case files and see what a couple owns. Many own a home that they must sell, and they are often willing to take a discount just to settle the assets and get out of the marriage quickly. Get to know some divorce attorneys and attend divorce court. You might find some good suspects there.

Suggestion # 37:   Estate and Probate Court

You can look up listings of deceased persons' assets in the public records. Contact the attorneys and the families and say, "Would you like to unload these properties quickly? I can help you out." You might find some deals.

Foreclosures

A foreclosure occurs when someone lends another person money to buy property, and the money is not paid back. Because the property provides the guarantee for the loan, the lender has the right to take possession of it, usually through a first, second, or third mortgage or a tax lien.

Who lends money? In our country, banks and mortgage companies provide most property loans. Some governmental agencies have the authority to impose a lien or judgment for nonpayment of funds owed (usually for taxes) and can foreclose on a property.

Suggestion # 38:   Bank or Mortgage Foreclosure Properties

Foreclosure properties are generally listed in the community's legal newspaper. In most cities and counties, lenders have to advertise in the legal or regular papers a few weeks before the sale occurs. You could also call the tax assessor's office or go to the register of deeds and ask for the list of the properties going into foreclosure.

Suggestion # 39:   Veteran's Administration Properties

The Veteran's Administration guarantees housing loans for veterans and publishes a list of houses it is foreclosing on. Sometimes these are good deals, and occasionally the VA offers very favorable financing. Check with mortgage brokers for details.

Suggestion # 40:   Housing and Urban Development (HUD) Properties

HUD guarantees some mortgage loans that banks make. It repossesses properties for unpaid mortgages, and you can bid on its foreclosed properties. Most real estate brokers and agents have access to lists of HUD foreclosures in the area. They could be a great place to find deals.

Suggestion # 41:   Lis Pendants

A *lis pendant* is a judgment or lien. When a creditor is awarded a judgment or lien against you in the courts, they can file a lien against your property. A book in the local property tax office lists all the lis pendants in that community. In Nashville, there are about $80 million worth of judgments against properties listed. People who have liens against their properties just might be motivated sellers, willing to sell to you at a discount. But be very careful. Get a collection attorney to handle it for you because of all the laws involved. You'll want to protect your interests well in the courts.

Special Sales

Good and great deals become available through special sales like the ones listed below.

Suggestion # 42:   Auctions

In addition to the auctions listed in the newspaper, look for other auction companies in the Yellow Pages. When you go driving for dollars, you will see signs about upcoming auctions. Call every auction company and get on their announcement lists, so that whenever they hold auctions, they'll send you notices for auctions of commercial properties, houses, apartment buildings, land, and so on. Attend all auctions that offer properties; you might find a great deal.

Suggestion # 43:   Preforeclosure Sales

I don't particularly like to buy at foreclosure sales. The owners have the property locked up, so you can't see the house or walk around inside and determine the extent of the needed repairs. I prefer to buy *before* the foreclosure sales by running an ad that says, "Home-Saver Program. Avoid foreclosure." This way, motivated sellers call you. How's that for marketing your business? They come to you! So buy before foreclosure.

When people have to go into foreclosure on their homes, it's because they have too much debt, or can't pay off their debts. As they realize this, they tend to follow a pattern. The first thing they do is call a lender and try to borrow more money. (What's the first thing a drunk does? Tries to get a drink.) The mortgage company tells them they can't get a new loan. Then they go to a real estate agent and try to sell their house within two weeks. The agent usually says it can't be sold that quickly. Then they'll go to their financial planner or accountant or banker and say they're in trouble, asking what actions they should take.

Your best bet is to network with all these professionals. They learn about debt situations well ahead of foreclosure. I know it works; I make $60,000 to $80,000 every year using this idea.

Suggestion # 44: Short Sales

For the first time in 30 to 40 years, some banks are discounting their mortgages. This is called a *short sale.* The Federal National Mortgage Association (FNMA, or Fannie Mae) and the Federal Home Loan Mortgage Corporation (FHLMC, or Freddie Mac) will accept 82 percent of what they think the property is worth as a short sale. So if they've loaned $100,000, and you offer $50,000, they will reject your proposal. Some banks will take less—you need to find out what kind of loan you're dealing with.

To do a short sale, you've got to find the seller, take over the property, and get written permission to negotiate with the bank—easy stuff. Prepare a package for the bank with a broker's opinion of the property's worth. Or the bank will send someone to meet you. If you're going to buy a house that you think is worth $250,000, and you're going to meet the bankers you'd rather have a broker's opinion say that its worth is much lower. Comps are an art. You and your real estate agent must do this legally and ethically—show some lower comparable sales.

Say the house needs $10,000 in repairs. Show the bankers a long list of needed repairs with retail (rather than wholesale) prices, even though you might be able to get the repairs done for less.

The hardest part of doing short sales is finding who to talk to at the bank. The bank is going to give you the royal runaround—most people give up. I worked on one short sale for four months before I talked to the right person. This is the hardest part. I have learned to go right to the president or manager of the real estate owned (REO) or loss mitigation department.

Suggestion # 45:   Tax Sales

If people do not pay their property taxes, the government taxing entity will demand payment and force a tax foreclosure. You can buy the property at a tax sale, or, in certain states, you can buy a tax certificate for the amount of the back taxes. By using a certificate, you get interest on your money or on the property. Some tax certificates pay anywhere from 10 to 30 percent interest.

People buy at tax sales for two reasons:

- They hope to get the property for the price of back taxes. For example, if an owner owes $8,000 in unpaid property taxes on a $200,000 home and it goes to a tax sale, an investor ideally wants to buy it for $8,000, the amount of the back taxes. Of course, others may also be bidding on this home, which can raise the price significantly. Be careful not to overspend at a tax sale. Still, you can find good deals there.

- Many cities, counties, and states require by law that the taxes owed and the amount bid collect a good interest rate. In certain areas, every taxing authority has rules and laws governing how sales are run. Some require that as much as 20 to 30 percent interest be paid.

  For example, say the owner of a house worth $200,000 owes $8,000 in back taxes. You bid $8,000 with the intent of acquiring the house for the amount of taxes only. However, your city has a one-year right of redemption rule. This means that the homeowner has one year to pay back all the taxes and interest due, and redeem the property. Therefore, if your area's interest rate for tax liens is 20 percent, the homeowner can pay you $8,000 plus 20 percent to get the house back. If the homeowner does not pay you off within one year, you get to keep the $200,000 home. However, you cannot sell that house until the year is up.

Alternatively, you could get a property for the amount of the tax lien. You can also acquire houses by bidding on them at the foreclosure auction. The IRS also puts tax liens on property.

When you hear about a pending tax sale or foreclosure, you should to talk to the property owners well before it happens. Are they motivated to sell? Yes. Are they hard to talk to sometimes? Yes, definitely, because people have a psychological defense mechanism called *denial*. Sometimes people will say, "No, I don't want to talk to you. I'm going to win the lottery. Someone will show up at my door and give me a million dollars. I know it's going to happen, so leave me alone."

At any rate, in most cases, the things that are hardest to obtain are the sweetest, so work these foreclosures and preforeclosure tax sales and develop a good stream of income.

Be careful to check out these items when you buy at a tax sale:

- Be aware of how much the repairs could cost.
- Talk to your local attorney and find out whether you can get title insurance. In most states you can. But in Tennessee, for example, you can't. If I go to a tax sale in Tennessee and buy a house for $4,000, I can *use* the house—I can rent it; I can live in it. But I can't *sell* it. I can't get a loan, because I can't get title insurance. Always ask about title insurance.
- Find out about the *right of redemption,* which is different in every state. Some states have no right of redemption. Then, when you buy a house at a tax sale, it's yours. You can get title insurance; you can sell it, buy it, refinance it. In other states, the owner has up to a year, sometimes two, to pay the back taxes, plus interest, and get the home back. This leaves you sitting out there for a year—it could be your house, or it might not be, if the old owner comes up with the money.
- Find out what the interest rate is. Some states pay 10 to 18 percent of any money you spent.

Suggestion # 46: Pretax Sales

Contact motivated sellers before they go to the tax sale. Get the list, call the owners, and write them letters. Offer them your home-saver program,

Make Sure the Title Is Good

Can you be sure you will get a good title at any of these sales? Who do you rely on to give you answers? I recommend that you work with experts from a reputable title company. Also, get an attorney who understands foreclosures and does thorough research. You do not have to understand title and foreclosure law; you do have to know how to talk to people who can answer title questions correctly for you.

and say, "Let me take care of this problem for you and stop the auction." They're in denial, and everyone is calling and writing them, so it's competitive. But you can get them out of debt, pay their back taxes, and take over the house.

I go to tax sales for one reason: to meet buyers. If you go to enough sales, you'll find a deal, although the sales can be highly competitive. Investors tend to go to the big cities. In Houston there are 3,000 tax sales on the second day of the month. Nashville has 800 properties once every quarter. Everybody's out there. The big banks are coming in and buying the tax liens. It's a great business, but it's very competitive. In the smaller towns and in some states where the population is low, the tax assessor's office has a list of properties they've taken back that are sitting on the shelf. The most successful investors are going to small towns, asking the tax officers what properties they have on the shelf, and achieving good results.

The Top-10 Real Estate Mistakes We Make Every Day

Check this list every day and see which mistakes you are making, then *stop* doing them. If you avoid these 10 mistakes in particular, you will dramatically increase your efficiency and success.

Make a copy of these pages, keep them by your desk, and review them throughout each day.

Top Mistake #1: Not Making a List Each Morning of Your Priorities and What You Intend to Accomplish That Day

Go ahead and create that list right now. You'll find it's the best way to control your day.

Doing this will dramatically increase your ability to get the most out of the time you spend on your real estate investment business. Don't let what's going on in the outside world distract you. Check off each activity as you finish it. And do this every day.

Activities I Will Accomplish Today

Top Mistake #2: Not Reviewing Your Activities List at the End of Every Day

Close every working day by checking over your list and seeing how much you actually accomplished. Decide how you will improve on the successes of the day. Ask yourself: How can I improve my business skills? My time management skills? Write down your answers.

I Can Improve My Business and Be More Successful By

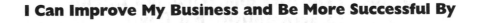

_____

_____

_____

_____

Top Mistake #3: Not Trying to Find a Deal Every Day

You make all of your short-term (wholesaling, lease-optioning, referral fees, buying and brokering notes, and private money lending), medium-term (buying, fixing, and selling; lease-optioning), and long-term (buying, renting, and holding) profits when you find good deals.

One deal can be worth as much as what people who work for salaries earn all year. Another deal can be worth a life's fortune. So what are you going to do today to find a deal?

Here are a few examples of action items:

- Run an I Buy Houses ad.
- Put up signs.
- Drive for dollars.
- Call on For Rent ads.
- Call on For Sale by Owner ads.
- Call on foreclosures.
- Network with others in the real estate business.

What I Will Do to Find a Deal Today

_____

_____

_____

_____

_____

_____

Top Mistake #4: Not Making an Offer Today

If you never make an offer, you won't have any real estate in your portfolio. If you use proper disclosures and contingency clauses, you incur almost no risk when you make offers. The most successful real estate investors put together a lot of offers. Go ahead—get started.

Offers I Will Make Today

_____

_____

_____

_____

_____

Top Mistake #5: Not Having an Organized Folder System and Not Using a Bulletin Board

It's important that you set up an organized system for your real estate investment business. For years, I recorded all of my potential deals and contacts on yellow sticky notes. Most of them landed below the seat in my car! What a mistake!

Now, I use a Palm Pilot personal digital assistant (PDA), a folder for each property, a to-do folder that I go through each day, a folder for bills to pay, and bulletin boards in my property management office to keep track of what is going on.

Go buy your office supplies today, and get organized. Write down the system you will use and follow it faithfully.

What I Need to Set Up My Tracking System

Top Mistake #6: Not Setting Up and Abiding by Strict Office Hours

Whether you work part-time or full-time as a real estate investor, you need to keep office hours. If you do not follow this policy, your personal life, family life, and spiritual life will all suffer. The strangest part is that you will feel more stressed out and probably make less money if you plug away, working too many hours.

Remember, one of the reasons you chose real estate investing is to enjoy more freedom and flexibility with your time. Setting and keeping office hours are key components in accomplishing that.

I Work in My Office during These Days and Hours

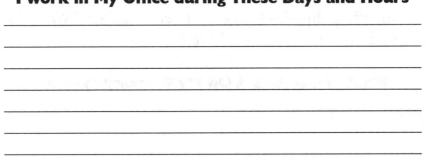

Top Mistake #7: Not Duplicating What Has Worked for You in the Past

What have you accomplished that has been successful? Working with real estate agents? Networking? Buying and selling foreclosures? Examine your successes, and let them lead the way to future successes. Be specific, so you will remember them. Your objective each day is to write down what is working and do more of it.

Activities That Have Been Successful So Far

_____

_____

_____

_____

_____

Look at that list, then simply do more of those activities. If a real estate agent found you a good deal, call that person back and explain that you want more deals like those. Call lots of other agents, too.

Human nature likes change, so it's tempting to overlook what works in anticipation of something new. I encourage you to focus, set up, and duplicate what's already working for you.

Top Mistake #8: Not Spending at Least 30 Minutes a Day on Improving Your Knowledge and Skills

The most successful people in the world always seem to make time to study, learn, and improve themselves. I commend you for reading this book and others in the field of real estate investing. However, you and I, like everyone else, seem to be extremely busy these days. As soon as we wake up, the phones, faxes, and e-mails start. Daily job, home, and family responsibilities take over our time. That's why it's critical to schedule at least 30 minutes each day to study new real estate skills and techniques. You may benefit from reading my other books, *Secrets of Buying and Selling Real Estate . . . Without Using Your Own Money* and *Unlimited Riches: Making Your Fortune in Real Estate Investing.* I have also written

Secrets of a Millionaire Real Estate Investor and *Secrets of a Millionaire Landlord.* I read almost every real estate investing book imaginable. They always reinforce what I know and give me ideas for new approaches.

Imagine if you read every single day—within a few years, you would be an expert. Remember, though, that studying is just the first step. The real test is in applying and testing what you learn from the books you read.

I Will Read and Study These Real Estate Books

Top Mistake #9: Not Thanking Someone Today Who Has Helped You Become Successful

This may sound strange, but consistently thanking people who have assisted you will help you become more successful. So often, people are so busy that they don't take the time to acknowledge what they have and, more important, those who have helped them.

Perhaps you can think of a friend, family member, teacher, spiritual leader, or business associate who has helped you. Do something special for that person: Buy a card, send a gift, write an e-mail, or make a phone call. Do this every day for 30 days, and you will find that people will respond to you more positively than ever.

Go ahead. Write down their names and contact them today.

I Will Say Thank You Today To

_____

_____

_____

_____

_____

_____

_____

_____

_____

_____

_____

_____

Top Mistake #10: Not Reminding Yourself Every Day of the Big Picture

Every day, write down the reasons why you are in this business. Use pictures, toys, or funny reminders that will keep you inspired about your business goals and activities.

If your goal is to make a certain amount of money, keep track of it. Make a poster with your goal clearly marked, and map your progress as you go.

If you want to purchase the car of your dreams, get a toy one that looks like the one you want, and place it on your desk where you can see it while you're working.

If your heart is set on taking a vacation, put up some travel posters or brochures for your desired destination on your bulletin board.

If you want more time with your loved ones or want to contribute more time to a charitable group, block out several hours on your calendar.

Remind yourself of what's important to you each day, so that when someone doesn't call you back, or a deal falls through, you won't be tempted to give up. You will keep moving toward your goal.

My Big Picture Reasons and Goals

Robert's Six Basic Rules
of Negotiation

I'd like to let you in on some of the secrets of the most successful real estate investors around the world. If you use these secrets—as countless other successful real estate investors have—you'll make thousands of extra dollars on every deal. Perhaps you won't get everything you ask for, but multiply your successes over all the deals you'll be making in the next 5 or 10 years. Good negotiation is a skill that will pay off.

Basic Rule # 1: Never Mention a Number until You Absolutely Have To

When talking with a motivated seller, ask, "What are you looking to get for this house? How did you come up with that number?" Keep asking questions. In negotiations, the first person to mention a number usually loses.

Here's an example. You're looking at a house you think is worth $200,000 and you'd likely buy it for $160,000. You call the seller, who says, "I'm going through a divorce. I need to move out of town. I'm behind on my mortgage payments." If the seller then asks you what you'd pay for it and you say $160,000, he or she will respond, "Great. Write it up."

You might feel good about that and proceed with the sale. However, a better approach is to respond to the seller's "How much would you pay?" question by asking, "What is the absolute rock-bottom price you'd take for your house today?" Then stop talking, and let the silence between you hang heavy. People don't like silence; they crave to fill it up.

Chances are, the seller will come back with, "Well, my rock-bottom price is $154,000." Bingo. In your mind, you were willing to pay $160,000. You just used this first rule to save another $6,000.

But don't close the conversation there. Make some grunting noises. Sigh. Frown. Then say, "Ummm, can you do any better?" That's the magic phrase: "Can you do any better?" Then stop again, pause, and let the silence work in your favor.

The seller may come back with, "Well, $154,000 really is my bottom number, but I would take $153,000." Miraculously, you just saved another $1,000 in that one minute of silence. Since that worked, go for it a third time and say, "Well, really, can you do any better than that?"

The seller might be getting frustrated by this time and may reply, "Hey, that's it. I'm done. You asked me for my rock-bottom price three times. That's it."

At this point, you can break the tension and say, in a chuckling way, "Well, for the fourth time, can you do any better?" Then smile and laugh. Have fun with it and see what happens.

Once the seller starts the negotiations by stating a price, you can come back with a much lower number. I always state my offers in odd numbers, just to be different. So if the seller offers $153,000, I come back with, "Well, I would like to give you $146,418."

That odd number can throw the seller off guard. The seller thinks you're working with a secret formula, or that you know something he or she doesn't know. The seller looks puzzled. Then he or she is likely to rebound and say, "Let's split the difference." The seller follows by offering $152,500. You follow with a number even lower than that—an odd number again.

This process may seem uncomfortable, but I guarantee that 80 or 90 percent of the time, you'll save thousands of dollars using this approach.

Basic Rule # 2: Ask Questions

If you're talking, you're not learning. In a negotiation process, you want to learn as much as you can. If you must say something, choose your words carefully. The fewer words you use, the better off you are!

Let your talking be in the form of questions. When talking about price, ask, "Why that price? How did you come up with that number?" Be sure to frame your questions so you get the answers you want. People are more likely to respond to questions with "no" than "yes," so pose questions that elicit a "no" but go in your favor. For example, "Is there any reason why you couldn't consider this offer?" If the seller says no to this question, move on to your proposal. It helps to be constantly reading the seller's body language, too. Body gestures often reveal answers that contradict what is said, so be aware of that.

Basic Rule # 3: Determine What the Seller Plans to Do with Any Cash That Changes Hands during This Transaction

Knowing the seller's plans could affect the negotiations. Maybe the seller just needs enough to pay off the mortgage and nothing more. It helps to know that.

Basic Rule # 4: Find Ways to Have the Seller Cover the Most Expenses Possible

The standard buyer's contract that you've prepared should spell out that the seller will pay all the closing costs and attorney's fees. Find ways to have the seller cover the most expenses possible.

Basic Rule # 5: Get It in Writing

Once you come to terms on the sale, get the details in writing, and get that paper signed. Until you have a signed contract, you have nothing.

Basic Rule # 6: Keep the Promises You Make

Promises are the foundation of your reputation, and you want that reputation to be golden.

Other Ways of Negotiating

If you don't like to negotiate or talk to people—if you're uncomfortable in these interactions—just write up a contract and mail it instead of negotiating over the phone or in person. That contract will be your offer. Make it a low offer, and include a contingency clause so you can get out of the deal if the property's in bad shape. Send out a lot of offers and follow them with phone calls.

When going into a negotiation, do your best to be relaxed when you walk into the room. For the first 5 or 10 minutes, talk about anything except the deal at hand. Ask about their families, if they like to travel, what their goals are, how they spent the weekend, and so on. If tension arises during the negotiations, soften it with a smile or a good-natured joke. A friend of mine often says, "I only want to offer you $2 for your house when it's worth $200,000." Then he'll say, "Just kidding. I'll offer you $3." This kind of banter lightens up the process.

Advanced Two-Step Negotiation

In my standard buyer's contract, I give myself 90 to 100 days—even 120 days—to close. Say you have three months to close on a real estate transaction and sign a contract with the seller. After the close, you're going to flip the property. But just two weeks after you set up the arrangement to buy the house, you line up a new buyer for that house. In this situation, why wait for three months to finalize the deal at closing?

First, verify that your buyer has the cash to complete the transaction, and, if everything checks out, set a closing date with that person. Then call the original seller and propose a two-step negotiation. Say, "As you know, we have about 85 days left to close on that house at $100,000. Is there any possibility that you could use the cash sooner than in 85 days?" What are the chances that the seller will say yes? Very high. Then you ask, "What would it be worth to you if I could give you all or most of the cash for that house in the next week or so? Given that, what's the least amount of money you would take for the house? Would you be interested in closing sooner and giving me a discount?" The seller responds, "Well, yes, possibly. How much were you thinking?"

Now, Basic Rule #1 states: Never mention a number until you absolutely have to. Instead of making an offer, say, "What's the least amount of cash you'd take if we could close in the next four or five days? Would closing sooner help you out?" You've just asked a question that will probably elicit a yes.

However, the seller might respond by saying, "I really need my whole $100,000." You reply, "Well, you'll get the full $100,000 in 85 days. But having cash in your hands sooner can add value to your money. What if I could get you the cash in four or five days? How much would you take?" At this point, stop and let the silence work for you.

If the seller answers with, "Okay, $99,000," you've just saved an extra $1,000. If he says nothing, ask again two or three times. If the seller won't mention a number, say, "If we can close in the next four or five days, would you take $92,826?"

The seller responds, "No way. Not that amount. But I would take $97,000."

You reply, "Can you do any better? Would you take any less? Would closing early help you out?"

The seller might come back with, "Well, $96,000 is the absolute rock-bottom price. The lowest."

Again say, "Well, can you do any better?"

The seller says, "I told you, that's it: $96,000. I'm not going lower. I'm getting mad here."

Then you say, "Well, I'd be more than glad to give you $93,418."

The seller might then say, "Well, let's split the difference at $95,000."

Okay. Now that you've come to an agreement, follow Basic Rule #5: Get it in writing!

Remember, whenever you're about to pay off a loan or mortgage early, always seek to negotiate a discount using this process. It will save you thousands over the years.

Guidelines for Successful Negotiating

- Ask kind and understanding questions; use them to gather information. Probe until you fully understand the seller's situation.

- Listen carefully to the answers, but remember to listen to and trust your inner (gut) feeling too.

- Identify what the seller really needs and what his or her motivation is through sensitive questioning and listening. Learn to describe the benefits of your offer in terms of the seller's needs.

- There are as many potential solutions as there are needs. Use your experience and your creativity! Offer no more than is necessary to fulfill those needs.

Valuable Rules to Improve Your Negotiating Skills

- The one who mentions price or terms first loses.

- Find ways to have the seller cover the most expenses possible.

- Use questions. Avoid declarative sentences.

- When someone answers "No," ask "Why not?"

- Promises are the foundation of your reputation. Make promises slowly and thoughtfully.

- Frame your questions to get the answers you want. People are much more motivated to respond with "no" than "yes." Make that "no" mean "yes" by posing your question: *"Is there any reason why you couldn't consider _____?"* If "no" is the answer you get, move on to your proposal.

- Be aware of body language—your own and the seller's. It reveals subconscious thoughts and feelings.

- Never be afraid of silence. Once you have asked a question, *wait* for the answer, no matter how long it takes. Remember, if you are talking, you are not learning. If you must say something, choose your words carefully.

- Never burn bridges. Those who become angry get out of control and almost always lose.

- Determine whether the seller needs all the cash now. Use that knowledge to your advantage.

- If the deal suits your needs, get a contract (subject to verification of the information) or an option for a period of time long enough to verify every detail.

- If the deal doesn't suit your needs, always pursue an option. This will give you time to rethink your position and see if someone else might like the opportunity.

Lease Optioning as a Money-Making Strategy

One of the best ways to get started making money in real estate is lease optioning. You can lease-option a single family home, a duplex, a triplex, a condominium complex, a resort property, and more. In fact, you can even lease-option apartment buildings to other investors.

What are the advantages and disadvantages of making a rent-to-own deal versus owning and renting property?

Advantages of Lease Optioning

- When you rent out a property, the deposit money belongs to the tenants; you hold it for them in a separate bank account and pay interest on that money. When tenants move out of your property and leave it in acceptable condition, you have to give back their deposit money. With lease optioning, you keep the deposit, which is called *option money*. If the tenants exercise their option to buy the property, that option money is applied toward the selling price. But if they walk away from the agreement and don't buy the property, or if they don't pay the rent on time, or don't do the things they agreed to do, *you* get the option money. Plus, you are not limited by state law on how much option money you can ask for, as you are with rental deposits.

- The amount of rent you can ask for depends on current market conditions. However, by giving people the benefit of renting to own, you can ask for, and often get a monthly payment that's higher than the going rental amount.

- With property rentals, you have one source of profit—the monthly rent. With lease optioning, you have three ways to make a profit: the option money, the rent, and appreciation on the sale. (See section titled The Three Lease-Option Profit Centers that follows.)

- When you rent out your property, you are responsible for all repairs (except any damage caused by your tenants)—one of the biggest complaints landlords have about owning property. A lot of your money can go toward repairs and upkeep, in addition to a lot of your time that you spend arranging for repairs. With lease optioning, the lease optioners are responsible for the majority of repairs. You've just stepped out of the minor repair business, though owners are usually responsible for major problems such as repairing roofs and replacing water heaters.

- When tenants move into a place they don't own, they don't tend to take the best care of it. They think that because it's not their property, they don't have to treat it as well as if they owned it. It's natural human behavior. Even if your tenants are the nicest people in the world, they'll make little effort to clean up messes and make minor repairs. With lease optioning, the pride of ownership that people feel about the place they live and will soon own proves to be a huge advantage. They'll fix up the place, make extra upgrades, plant flowers and bushes, take care of the landscaping, and much more.

■ Some investors may view selling their lease-optioned properties as a disadvantage because they don't own them for a long time. But consider this: Say you find a house worth $110,000 in today's marketplace and pay $80,000 for it. You lease-option that house for $115,000, which is the selling price when the house is sold a year or two down the road. In that time, you'll make $35,000. Is making $35,000 really a disadvantage? It's an advantage, because you can use that profit to find more deals and make more money.

■ When you own property and rent it out, you can depreciate the buildings and write off all related expenses on your tax returns. Having a rental business can reduce your taxable income substantially. You may complain and say, "If I buy a house at $80,000 and sell it in two years at $115,000, I'll have to pay a lot of taxes on that capital gain." Personally, I love to pay taxes, because that means I'm making a profit. Investors don't go broke when they're making a profit! So be glad you're making money—and enjoy the benefits of writing off a lot of the travel, meals, and other expenses related to your real estate business. (Please check with your accountant and attorney to make sure you're following the letter of the law in this regard.) *Note:* You do not pay taxes on the option money until that option expires or until your lease optioners exercise their option.

Disadvantages of Lease Optioning

- Beware of repairs and potential vacancies. If people don't exercise their option to buy your place and move out instead, you may have to deal with a lot of damage. However, you should have received enough up-front money to cover any repairs required.

- You have to realize that until your lease optioners close the deal and buy, they are still renters. They may do damage and cause problems that tenants typically turn to landlords for. However, the conditions of your lease-option agreement should minimize the problems.

- Although you don't need a lot of capital or credit to make lease-option deals, you do need a lot of potential deals and a business plan to follow to ensure that each deal is profitable.

The Three Lease-Option Profit Centers

With lease optioning, you basically benefit from having three profit centers.

- Number one is the difference in up-front or option money, which means the lease optioners pay you more money than you pay the original sellers.

- Number two is the difference in the monthly spread. Say you pay out $500 a month in mortgages and receive $1,000 a month in rent. This means you make $500 a month. Your agreement may require that you apply some of that money toward a down payment.

- Number three is the difference between the amount you paid for the house (e.g., $80,000 in this example) and what you eventually sell it for (e.g., $115,000).

The Sandwich Lease Option

If you find a property you want, you can lease it instead of buying it. Yes, instead of borrowing money, buying the property, being on title, assuming the liability, and putting your credit at stake, you can control the property through a lease with an option to buy. You can lease the property from the owner, then turn around and arrange a "sandwich" lease option with the eventual buyer. This way, you don't put a lot of money down and you haven't borrowed any. You've only signed a lease. Then, if the world comes to an end or the real estate market nosedives, you're not responsible for paying a mortgage. You can always walk away from a lease if something bad happens, though I don't recommend it except in extraordinary situations. However, by definition, you're not *obligated* to buy; rather, you have an *option* to buy.

Here's an example of a sandwich lease option.

Say you're able to lease an executive-type home for $1,700 a month. You negotiate with the seller for a five-year option to buy the property at any time for $170,000. (You could even match your option price to the value of the seller's mortgage so the price goes down as the mortgage is paid off.) After doing your homework, you learn that an executive home like this one rents for $2,500 to $2,700 a month. Next, you run a test ad in the local paper without stating a price. It says Rent to Own, Easy Qualifying, Become a Home Owner on Easy Terms, and so on. Run this ad in the local paper to see how many phone calls you get. If you get very few calls, reword the ad and run it again. If you get lots of calls, then you're dealing with a high-demand market.

When an interested person calls and says, "I'd love to rent to own a house. How much is the rent?" answer by saying, "How much are you looking to spend?" If the reply is $2,900, that's better than the amount you had in mind. You respond by saying, "Congratulations. We can rent it to you for $2,900." Your lease-option agreement is $1,700 a month, so you'll be $1,200 ahead.

Then the caller asks about the option money amount and the sale price. You respond by asking, "How much are you looking to put down?" The more money they're willing to put down, the more serious they are, the more you're protected, and the more care they'll take once they live in the home. You can formalize the process by asking callers to complete the form shown in Figure D.1, which helps you qualify prospects.

Although you might have a number in mind, your job is to keep posing questions. Ask the caller, "How much cash do you have?" They might come back with, "We've got $14,000 for a down payment." Or they might say, "We've only got $500 as option money." If that happens, you know they can't afford to pay the monthly rent, so you quickly move on to another caller.

At a minimum, I recommend requiring at least two or three months' worth of rental payments as option money—more, if you can get it. If someone only has $1,000, you can predict that you'll have problems.

Lease Option Prospect Qualify Form

Name _____   Date/time _____
Phone _____   Regarding rating _____
2nd applicant name _____   Other applicants _____
                                        Pets   Y or N

  I. Are you looking to rent or own? _____   Have you seen the property? Y or N
  2. Where do you live now? _____   How long there? _____
  3. Is it a house or apartment? _____
  4. How much do you pay now? _____   Have you ever been evicted or late to pay?
  5. Is your landlord aware that you will be moving? Y or N
  6. Employer/position _____   How long there?____ Gross earnings ____
  7. Spouse's employer/position _____   How long there?____ Gross earnings ____
  8. How is your credit? _____   How is spouse's credit? _____
  9. When can you move in? _____   Most you can pay per month? _____
10. How much money do you have to put down on your new home? _____
Tax return? Y or N   Can you pay extra per month to build up a down payment? Y or N
The bank requires this form, and it will help us work out a down-payment plan.

We want you to succeed in having your own home!

Figure D.1   Qualification form for lease-option prospects.

Over time, I've found that the more people can put down, the better they will pay, and the easier they'll be to work with.

In this example, you ideally want lease optioners who are willing to put down $7,000 to $8,000 and lease the home for more than $2,600 a month. Your agreement gives them a one-year option to buy the home at any time. It's been appraised at $200,000, although appraisals can vary significantly. I recommend that you take a conservative route and option the property for $210,000 to $215,000. Remember, you have an agreement with an option to buy it from the original owner any time in the next five years for $170,000.

Once you have an agreement lined up, be sure to disclose what you're doing in writing for the benefit of everyone involved. You could get into trouble if you don't, because some people have been accused of fraud when they lease-option properties. Your best defense is disclosure. Therefore, tell the original owner that you're going to rent it, lease-option it, or sell it for a profit. State that clearly in writing. Be sure to add, "I don't represent you or your interests." Then, when you lease-option it to the people who will live in it, disclose to them that you may or may not have clear title. After all, who knows what could happen in the process of buying the property from the original seller? A divorce. A bankruptcy. Anything. That's why you may not be able to pass clear title to the property.

In the agreement with your buyers, also state in writing, "I don't represent you or your interests." This is critical, because if there's a title problem, and you haven't disclosed your role as an investor and the possibility that you might fail to secure an unencumbered title to the property, your buyers could sue you, declaring, "You didn't tell us you had a lease option. We thought you owned it and could pass clear title." It's perfectly legal and ethical to lease-option property if you disclose to everyone in writing what you're doing. (Please consult your lawyer or accountant before acting on this, because rules vary in different cities and counties.)

By using a sandwich lease option like this, you bring in hundreds of dollars every month. The original owner is responsible for major repairs, insurance, and property taxes. The end user takes care of minor repairs and puts money toward the purchase price every month. And you make it possible for people to own their home.

When Your Investment Business Needs Help: How to Build the Perfect Team

*T*his chapter was written by Rose-mary Taugher, who has over 20 years' experience setting up financial and administrative systems, most recently for real estate investors. Formerly a chief financial officer of successful young companies in central Europe, she is now a real estate investor herself.

There comes a point in your investing career when you can no longer manage all your investments and activities by yourself, and you find it necessary to bring in someone else for help. This decision will have far-reaching effects—it will either make your life wonderful or make your life very stressful.

Making the Decision

There are a variety of ways to get help. You can bring in a partner; you can hire outside advisors to take some of the workload off you; or you can hire someone, either on payroll or as an independent contractor.

No matter what route you take, you absolutely *must* decide first of all just exactly *what* it is that you want to pass off to someone. Sit down at your keyboard or with a pen and piece of paper, then list *all* the tasks you do in a month. Really take some time with this, and list everything you can think of. It helps tremendously to spend several weeks writing down everything you do each day, and noting how much time you spend doing it. This way, not only do you know what you are doing with your days, but you also know how long it takes to get those things done.

After you have listed all the tasks and the time each one takes, prioritize the list according to these categories:

- On a scale of 1 to 10, how important is that task to your business?
- What skill level is required to complete the task?
- What do you really like doing?
- What do you really hate doing?
- What are you the best at doing?
- What are your weakest areas?

Then ask yourself:

- How much would you have to pay someone to do various tasks? (Check out local pay rates.)

- What is your budget to pay someone; what can you afford right now?

After you've completed this exercise, you'll recognize a pattern of tasks, and you will have a much clearer idea of what you can and want to give away. You'll also know what it will cost you, and how much you have available to cover those costs.

Bringing in a Partner

One of the easiest things to do on a short-term cash-flow basis is to bring in a partner. Normally, a partner comes in with cash or skills and services to offer, and you'll have immediate relief. If you choose the right partner, it can be great fun. You can move ahead really quickly, you can get moral support, and you can learn from your partner. You can potentially do things and achieve a scale of growth that you never could alone.

The downside is that you share not only expenses and tasks, but your net profit, as well. This can be a very expensive solution to what may be a short-term problem. You also have to share power and decision-making authority. Bringing in a partner is nearly like getting married—you are with each for better or worse, you are totally liable for each other's actions, and it can be very messy and expensive to get a "divorce."

If you do decide to go the partnership route, take time to work up a job description for each one of you. Decide who does what, who gets to make which decisions, and how you will resolve conflicts and differences. Then protect yourselves by forming a limited liability company (LLC) or a limited partnership, depending on what's most effective in your state. Check with an attorney on this. Get some references from your local real estate investors club.

As part of establishing your LLC or limited partnership, you must prepare an operating agreement or partnership agreement. In this agreement, spell out everything you've agreed on, from who does what, who signs what, and who gets paid what to how you share profits and losses. Be sure to include your job descriptions and a buyout agreement in case you decide to end the partnership.

Limited partnerships and LLCs are inexpensive to establish, so it often makes sense to form separate partnerships for each deal. I know one investor who frequently makes deals with other investors and simply uses the same LLC, buying out the other partner each time.

If you choose not to form a partnership, the next thing to consider is how well you supervise people. If you just hate it—if you dread correcting people and dislike the whole idea of managing employees—consider hiring outside services.

You can take several different approaches, as noted in the following sections.

Choosing and Working with Professionals

In-House or Outside Advisors

First identify exactly what tasks you need help with or want to have someone do. Be specific and write down all the tasks.

One option is to hire someone who has good qualifications but isn't skilled enough to do the full job alone. This person can work under the supervision of an outside advisor. Perhaps the outside advisor can help your staff person set up the system and work through the first several jobs, then later can conduct periodic reviews of the staff person's work.

Another option is to have all the work done by an outside firm. Generally, you get what you pay for. When an advisor is young, new to the field, or just inexperienced, the price normally will be significantly cheaper, but quality and professionalism may be seriously lacking. Save crises, high-profile situations, and critical issues for highly qualified advisors. Remember, this is your business and your money that you are entrusting to someone else.

When You've Decided to Get Outside Help

- Get three or four references. Always, *always* check references! Always ask the same questions on each reference, and make notes on each reference you get.

- Ask successful real estate investors whom they use. Get the names and telephone numbers. Ask these investors if they are happy with the services they receive.

- Ask one of your current professional advisors to recommend someone. Professionals often work in teams. This can be very good for you, or very bad. If you choose badly, your problems can be multiplied greatly, but if you choose well, you can save a great deal of time and money, with fewer things falling through the cracks.

When You've Compiled a Good List of Names

Conduct personal interviews with each potential candidate. Write up a list of questions you need to ask and use the list as a guideline. Ask each candidate the same questions, and *make notes* on each one. Then take a few minutes after each interview to write down your initial thoughts and feelings. Review your notes and record your impressions again after two or three days. Then, at the end of the interview process, do a final review.

Questions to Ask and Things You Should Know

- How well do the candidates pay attention to detail? Take note of the appearance of their offices, and whether they meet you on time for the appointment or keep you waiting. Ask about typical turnaround times for completing projects.

- What educational backgrounds do the candidates have? Ask specifically about education pertinent to the tasks you need done.

- What are their skill levels? How many years of experience do they have? What types of deals have they made? Do they have any specific experience with your types of needs?

- Are they required to have any professional licenses or accreditation? Is it up-to-date?

- If you're interviewing accountants, do the candidates have any experience in the real estate industry?

- How do they structure their fees? Have them explain their fees in great detail, and find out how you will be invoiced for their services.

- Will they have payment schedules?

- Do they require a retainer? How does their retainer system work? Can you save any money this way?

Identifying the Perfect Person

- When you've collected notes on several choices, take a good look at your list. Remember that there doesn't necessarily have to be one "perfect person." You can always decide to choose several people and use them for different tasks.
- What were the results of your interviews?
- Was it difficult to get an appointment?
- How were you treated during the interviews? Will they come to your place of business? Did they answer phones and deal with regular interruptions, or did you receive their full attention?
- Were questions answered completely and honestly (as far as you can tell)?
- Were their offices neat and organized, or messy and cluttered?
- Do they have support staff?
- Did they clearly explain fees, procedures, timelines, and the like? Do they have written policies on these?
- What did their references say? Did any of them seem guarded?
- Finally, trust your instincts! No matter how highly qualified the advisor, if you don't like the person, you won't work well together.

Start Small First

Once you choose an advisor, a good rule to follow is to use your new advisor for a small job first, before committing to anything bigger.

Beware of the following:

- Advisors who promise the moon.
- Unrealistic time schedules.
- Low fees.
- Advisors who allow your time to be interrupted.
- Government program advisors. Check their quality, because it varies wildly. Many advisors have no experience in running a business, and no particular education that's relevant to running a business.

When you've finally made the decision, write up a contract. Be sure all expectations and responsibilities are put on paper and signed by both parties.

Periodically review all professional advisor relationships. After several months or after several jobs, how do these advisors score on your original rating criteria? Are they doing a good job? How do you know?

Specify the results! Are you communicating your needs and your feelings on a regular basis and giving the advisor good feedback? A good advisor acts just like a close member of your team, and will get to know your business nearly as well as you do. This person can be a source of invaluable advice. Treat him or her well, and expect to be treated well in return.

Suggestions for Seeking Help

See Table E.1 for an outline of suggestions.

Table E.1 Suggestions for Selecting Help

Type of Help	Type of Business		
	Single Investor with Few Properties	Investors with Several or Many Properties and Investment Activities	Medium-Sized Investment Company
Accounting	Hire an outside advisor to do all tasks.	Hire a front-office person who does many tasks and is responsible for daily data entry; work is supervised by an outside advisor.	Hire one person just for accounting or set up a finance department as needed.
Legal	Hire an outside advisor to do all tasks.	Have an external lawyer prepare all contracts, creating a template as needed. Have a staff person prepare subsequent similar contracts, reviewed by the external lawyer.	Hire in-house legal staff.

Employees versus Independent Contractors

If you've decided you really need someone in-house and you're okay with managing people, you need to decide whether you're ready to have an employee or an independent contractor in your business. By far the best way to go, if you can, is to work with everyone as an independent contractor, as explained in the following paragraphs.

Here's what you should know before hiring.

Employees

The IRS has regulations covering who can actually be considered an independent contractor. These rules deal primarily with how much control you're able to exercise over the person. If you insist on a uniform or a dress code and a set schedule, and if you control every aspect of the person's work, that person is an employee. This means that you need to register with the IRS as an employer, get an employer ID number, and file regular payroll tax returns. You must withhold employee taxes and pay employer taxes on your payroll. You must carry disability insurance and establish rules about including employees in any benefit plan you offer. You are also exposed to a certain amount of liability regarding tasks the employee carries out on your behalf.

Independent Contractors

The easier way to go is to hire people on an independent contractor basis. In this case, contractors set their own schedules, work at their own locations (sometimes at yours), and most often work for more than one business. You instruct the independent contractor in what needs to be done and by when, and you pay that person to get it done. By working this way, you save the headaches of dealing with liability issues, payroll tax issues, and additional bookkeeping and payroll expenses.

Hiring Procedures

Now that you've made up your mind to hire someone, whether as an independent contractor status or as an employee, it's extremely important to start the relationship off on the right foot. Use the same procedures for either.

Job Description

Write up a short summary of what you are looking for (see the Sample Job Description and Sample Ad sidebars) and either put the ad in the paper or distribute it among other professionals and friends.

Interview Form

Once you start getting calls, make appointments and use a standard interview form for everyone. The questions you ask will uncover a great deal of information about the person in front of you (see the Sample Interview Questions sidebar). Even if you are short on time, pick a healthy number of questions out of the form and ask as many as you can. One of my personal all-time favorites is "If you were me, why would you hire you?" Some of the answers prove to be very revealing about a person's attitude and self-confidence.

Sample Job Description

- Part time bookkeeper-accountant, experienced, must know accounting through journal entries
- Willing to work as an independent contractor
- Willing to work in a home office
- Great personality, willing to work with fun clients who are in growing businesses, in real estate investment
- Accurate, fast, willing to learn, flexible
- Good people skills
- Willing and able to do some customer service for real estate investor (phones, follow-up)
- Willing and able to supervise others
- Interested in a growth position
- Pay level dependent on experience and qualifications

Looking for someone with a strong organizational, clerical, accounting, management, bookkeeping, and secretarial bent, and a touch of marketing skill thrown in. Must have good people skills. Must like numbers, people, and good organization as well as good attention to detail. Must be willing to work in a virtual office, love being part of a team, and work well with others. This part-time growth position is in the real estate investment industry. Salary depends on experience and qualifications.

You want to let the applicant know that you take your business seriously and that you expect your potential new helper to take it seriously as well. Even if you feel foolish at first, fill out the forms as completely as possible. You'll be astonished at how much information you will collect.

As soon as the interview is over, complete an overall assessment form (see Figure E.1). Don't wait to fill it out, because it's too easy to forget key things or let your impressions be clouded in subsequent interviews. Again, fill it out as completely as possible.

Sample Interview Questions for Employees

- What experience do you have in setting up office systems?
- What experience do you have in supervising others?
- What are your computer skills?
- What are your future plans and ambitions?
- Are you a self-starter?
- Do you consider yourself disciplined? Motivated?
- What motivates you?
- What skills do you have? Computer; 10 key; typing: _____
- What salary do you desire? Is hourly okay?

- Do you consider yourself organized?
- Are you able to work under pressure?
- Do you have references? Please provide three references.
- How important are benefits to you? What kind of benefits would you like?
- What experience do you have in answering phones, taking messages, and so forth?
- What experience do you have in running an office alone?
- How do you take criticism and stress?
- How did previous employers treat you?
- Have you helped increase sales? Profits? How?
- Have you helped reduce costs? How?
- In what type of position are you most interested?
- Why do you want to work for this company?
- What do you think determines a person's progress in a good company?
- What kind of supervision do you prefer?
- Do you like routine work?
- What is your major weakness?
- What types of people annoy you?
- What are your special abilities or skills?
- How do you feel about overtime work?
- In what ways will this company benefit from your services?
- If you were me, why would you hire *you*?

One Clear Choice

Take a day or two and let your thoughts settle. You'll be surprised at what will drift up into your conscious mind. Reread the assessments and questionnaires, then go with what your instincts tell you. You'll find there's usually one clear choice. Always be careful about your choices. Remember, you are entrusting this person with important aspects of

Applicant Assessment

Name _____

Position _____ Dept _____

Applicant source _____ Date _____

Interviewed by _____

Strengths	Weaknesses

Areas you are concerned about:

Areas in which more information is needed:

Figure E.1   Sample applicant assessment form.

Knowledge and experience:

Intellectual capacity (in relation to demands of job):

Motivation/interest in the job responsibilities and duties:

Personality (in relation to demands of the job) and ability to fit into the existing work group:

Smoking/nonsmoking:

Overall Assessment

For initial position: Outstanding / Above average / Average / Below average

Growth potential: Outstanding / Above average / Average / Below average

Recommended Action: (If rejected, give reason—be specific; use other side of paper.)

your business. It's your reputation, your livelihood, and your money. Run a credit check and a background check on your final choice, especially for someone who will be anywhere near your money.

Settling into the Relationship

Be clear about what you expect from the new person. You will already have prepared a job description, so be sure to go over it in great detail. Give clear directions, and allow time for training and for the inevitable learning curve. Just as with outside advisors, you'll get what you pay for. Unless you are really willing to train and you're good at it, consider paying more for an experienced person. It will save you a great deal of time and stress, and you should be out making deals anyway. Even in the short run, it will save money.

Take time to review the work daily until you are comfortable with the level of work and with the results you are getting. Even then, get weekly reports as a matter of policy.

If you have someone who is working with your money or your financial statements, take a course in reading and understanding financial statements for business owners. Make sure you have good internal controls set up, and that you follow them.

Living With Your Decision

Once you've made your decision and taken action, relax and enjoy the improvement. Remember that you took on a partner, hired an outside advisor, or hired an in-house person so you could do more of what you love doing and more of what makes you money. Just be sure to follow the procedures here and set up your internal controls.

Get weekly reports, keep in clear communication with each other, and enjoy your increased profits and your growing business.

About the Author

Rosemary Taugher has been working with entrepreneurs and investors in both Europe and the United States for many years. A teacher and speaker, her papers have been published at international conferences. In addition to her extensive background in accounting and taxes, she has managed large projects designing and implementing business management software installations. She is now a managing member of Compass Rose International LLC, a company that sets up practical business systems for real estate investors. She has written several home study courses for investors— from understanding financial statements, to managing cash flow, to creating a killer business plan, to figuring out the practical aspects of managing legal structures and asset protection. Check out her web site at *www.compassroseint.net* and get one of her free reports.

Robert Shemin, JD, MBA, is an active real estate investor who has bought or sold more than 400 properties. He's the best-selling author of *Secrets of Buying and Selling Real Estate . . . Without Using Your Own Money, Unlimited Riches: Making Your Fortune in Real Estate Investing,* and *Secrets of a Millionaire Real Estate Investor.* He also maintains a web site with useful tools and helpful advice for real estate investors at www.sheminrealestate.com.

A recognized real estate expert and seminar leader, he has appeared on national and syndicated television and on major-city talk radio shows. His appearances include the Montel Williams show and various programs on CBS and ABC. He has spoken to more than 10,000 real estate investors and frequently lectures at real estate associations around North America and in Australia and New Zealand.